UNDERSTANDING PRIMARY PHYSICAL EDUCATION

In order to become a more effective practitioner every teacher needs to have a sound understanding of the theoretical, social and historical context in which their work takes place. *Understanding Primary Physical Education* goes further than any other textbook in exploring the development of Physical Education teaching at the primary and elementary level, drawing together important research from across the educational and sociological literature.

The book goes beyond everyday teaching practice at an operational level to encourage students, trainee teachers and researchers to develop a critical understanding of policy, process and practice in primary Physical Education. By rooting everyday documents and everyday issues in a broader, connected educational and developmental landscape, this book challenges casual assumptions and encourages a better, more thoughtful teaching practice. It is an essential companion for any degree-level course in primary Physical Education.

Gerald Griggs is a Senior Lecturer in Physical Education and Sports Studies at the University of Wolverhampton, UK. Gerald trained as a primary teacher, specialising in Physical Education, before teaching in primary schools in the UK. Since moving into Higher Education he has published and presented widely on primary Physical Education and the sociology of sport.

UNDERSTANDING PRIMARY PHYSICAL EDUCATION

Gerald Griggs

Routledge
Taylor & Francis Group

LONDON AND NEW YORK

First published 2015
by Routledge
2 Park Square, Milton Park, Abingdon, Oxon OX14 4RN

and by Routledge
711 Third Avenue, New York, NY 10017

Routledge is an imprint of the Taylor & Francis Group, an informa business

British Library Cataloguing in Publication Data
A catalogue record for this book is available from the British Library

Library of Congress Cataloging-in-Publication Data
A catalog record for the this book has been requested

ISBN: 978-0-415-83570-1 (hbk)
ISBN: 978-0-415-83572-5 (pbk)
ISBN: 978-0-203-79491-3 (ebk)

Typeset in Bembo
by HWA Text and Data Management, London

Printed and bound by CPI Group (UK) Ltd, Croydon, CR0 4YY

CONTENTS

TABLES AND BOXES

Tables

Boxes

PREFACE

In my previous publication for Routledge, *An Introduction to Primary Physical Education*, I edited a text which comprised a congregation of the talents of those consistently writing, speaking and *specialising* in the delivery of primary Physical Education. The aim of that text was to be at the forefront of providing direction and high quality guidance for the delivery of a primary Physical Education curriculum.

However it became apparent during the writing of that text that a further contribution would be needed for those who are required to academically study the individual components of primary Physical Education practice and demand further sources to delve deeper into the underpinning bedrock of each area. Many such sources are located primarily within educational policy, educational theory and often sociological theory making them sometimes hard to access and disparate in nature. This book, *Understanding Primary Physical Education*, aims to sit next to or perhaps arguably above *An Introduction to Primary Physical Education* rooting key areas identified chapter by chapter in essential academic literature.

Given the time constraints placed upon professionals engaged within Physical Education and perhaps more broadly still, Primary Education, there is little wonder than many seek quick and practical solutions in their day-to-day lives. Unsurprisingly engagement with texts and current policy documents such as the National Curriculum for Physical Education remains at an operational level rather that at a critical one. By rooting the everyday documents and the everyday issues such as teaching in a broader, connected landscape, this book seeks to offer a deeper understanding for practitioners.

The current fashion within the Higher Education landscape to deliver 'bite size' experiences or modules also encourages quick and practical solutions for both educators and students despite concerns that such approaches limit the depth of learning desired. With further expectations placed on the levels of knowledge and understanding of those moving towards postgraduate study and training, and the renewed research interests across the globe into elementary- or primary-level Physical Education, it is of increased importance that a book such as *Understanding Primary Physical Education* provides a secure theoretical underpinning to those studying the subject area.

The book is arranged in eleven chapters and, to assist in a wider understanding of each of the chapters, key readings have been identified throughout. Furthermore, following the introduction, each chapter contains 'thought boxes' to highlight important aspects to reflect upon. It is hoped that by fully engaging in the text, readers will feel they have moved closer towards '*Understanding Primary Physical Education*'.

Gerald Griggs

ACKNOWLEDGEMENTS

To K.G. for your clarity of direction when I can't see the wood for the trees.

To M.G., K.L., G.W., R.M., N.O.L. and H.K., for creating the best environment within which to work and undertake projects such as this book.

To B.C. and B.G. for all your support and for always keeping my feet on the ground.

In addition, thanks must also be given to the team at Routledge for their continued support and patience.

ACRONYMS

AOTTs	adults other than teachers
BERA	British Educational Research Association
BMA	British Medical Association
CfE	Curriculum for Excellence
CL	cooperative learning
CPD	continuing professional development
ECM	Every Child Matters
DCMS	Department of Culture, Media and Sport
DfES	Department for Education and Skills
EYFS	Early Years Foundation Stage
FMS	fundamental movement skills
GCSE	General Certificate of Secondary Education
HMI	Her Majesty's Inspectorate
HMSO	Her Majesty's Stationery Office
ITE	initial teacher education
ITT	initial teacher training
LEA	local education authority
NACCCE	National Advisory Committee on Creative and Cultural Education
NCPE	National Curriculum for Physical Education
NGB	national governing body
OAA	outdoor and adventurous activities
OCC	Open Creativity Centre
OFSTED	Office For Standards in Education
PA	physical activity
PCK	pedagogical content knowledge

PDM	partnership development manager
PE	physical education
PEPAYS	Physical Education, Physical Activity and Youth Sport
PESSCL	Physical Education, School Sport and Club Links
PESSYP	Physical Education and Sport Strategy for Young People
PGCE	post graduate certificate of education
PLT	primary link teacher
PPA	planning, preparation and assessment
PSA	public service agreement
PSHE	personal, social, health and economic education
QCA	Qualifications and Curriculum Authority
QTS	qualified teacher status
SCITT	school-centred initial teacher training
SE	sport education
SSCo	school sport co-ordinator
SSP	school sport partnership
TGfU	teaching games for understanding
TSO	The Stationery Office
UNICEF	United Nations International Children's Emergency Fund
UK	United Kingdom
WHO	World Health Organization

1

INTRODUCTION

With time constraints placed upon busy professionals engaged within primary education, and more specifically still within Physical Education, there is little wonder why many seek quick and practical solutions in their day-to-day teaching lives. Capitalising on this state of affairs, many texts for primary Physical Education are still pitched as 'How to …' guides or as 'one size fits all' lesson plans. In reality of course pupils and teachers are not the same and consequently when 'How to …' guides do not work and lesson plans do not fit all, teachers can flounder. It was from this starting point that my previous publication for Routledge, *An Introduction to Primary Physical Education*, was developed. Comprising a congregation of the talents of those consistently writing, speaking and *specialising* in the delivery of primary Physical Education, the edited text set out to be at the forefront of providing direction and high quality guidance for the delivery of a primary Physical Education curriculum.

However, while writing that text it became apparent that at the same time that training for subjects such as Physical Education within primary courses was being reduced, further expectations were to be placed on trainees' levels of knowledge and understanding. Furthermore, with increasing numbers moving towards postgraduate study, and the renewed research interests across the globe into elementary or primary level Physical Education, it seemed of increased importance that a further book could provide a secure theoretical underpinning to those needing to further their understanding of primary Physical Education. In order to offer this level of understanding, further sources needed to be sought to delve deeper into the underpinning bedrock of each area. For this text, sources are located primarily within educational policy, educational theory and sociological theory.

Following this introduction, Chapter 2 concerns itself with locating Physical Education which is not as straight forward as it might first appear. Although many might be clear as to what they mean by 'Physical Education', a little reading reveals the term is something of a contested concept. In such circumstances understanding the broader landscape becomes essential rather than adopting a narrow focus. Furthermore, if we are therefore to comprehend *where* we and others currently stand and perhaps more importantly *why*, it is important to understand the key texts and narratives that impact upon such stances. Across the world, most, if not all of these are located within the fields of sport, education and health. Attention in this chapter turns to look at this complex and changing relationship that sport, education and health have with Physical Education in order to effectively locate it, and furthermore how this relationship has impacted at primary school level particularly within the UK. A further consideration of Physical Education's positioning within the wider movement culture also serves to highlight useful areas for critical discussion.

In Chapter 3, attention turns to examining Physical Education in the primary curriculum. Historically, the story of primary education within the United Kingdom has been comparatively short yet despite this, polarising viewpoints upon a highly contested terrain have wrestled for philosophical control of the primary curriculum. The key related documents underpinning these viewpoints are explained here which helps to further understand the first incarnation of the National Curriculum in England and Wales in 1991 of which Physical Education was named as a discrete subject. The further revisions of the primary curriculum which occurred in 1995, 1999 and most recently in 2014 are then explained with a commentary explaining the impact of first the Conservative government, the following Labour government and then latterly the coalition government (Conservative and Liberal Democrats) upon the curriculum content. What becomes evident here is the impact and influence that events or policies have had during the creation of the primary Physical Education curriculum, without understanding the appropriateness or impact that has resulted.

Chapter 4 reveals the disquiet about the value of teacher preparation that has been voiced for the past twenty years, particularly the training offered to primary level teachers to teach Physical Education. At a time of erratic and incoherent change in teacher education in the UK, in recent years the preparation of teachers has moved away from developing a critical insight into the role of pedagogy and retreated to a set of reductionist and functional competencies. Barriers to further the development of primary professionals here have been concerned with deficiency in time, attitude, a lack of subject knowledge and the resulting low levels of competence and confidence. The chapter explores how further the attainment for pupils in primary Physical Education might be raised.

Chapter 5 considers the often neglected underpinning of the day-to-day practice of those delivering primary Physical Education. Aspects within the broader pedagogical cycle of planning, teaching and assessment will form the focus for the content. Within this detail the text will consider elements such as teaching styles, models of delivery and the variety of assessments on offer within primary Physical Education.

Physical Education, as with other subject areas, needs to be led and directed within a school environment. However finding a clear direction has proved problematic against a backdrop of changing standards for teachers, the reduction in the advisory service, the making and breaking of school partnerships and the competitive market of outsourcing Physical Education. Chapter 6 charts how this role has changed considerably over the last two decades and considers how effective subject leadership might be provided.

Chapter 7 explores the concept of creativity within Physical Education, which has become something of a buzzword in contemporary education. Policy documentation shows an overt commitment to the development of creativity, yet the realities within primary schools appear somewhat different. This chapter looks at the environment and practice within schools and suggests that teachers can do much to encourage what is described as 'small c' creativity. Specifically this chapter makes recommendations for how this could manifest itself within everyday primary Physical Education.

The phrase 'health and well being' has become a fashionable addition to our common vocabulary in the 21st century. Yet oddly, despite the unabated adoption of the phrase, there remains significant ambiguity around the definition, usage and function of 'health and well being' in the public policy realm and in the wider world. However at a policy level it is the widespread adoption of the term within education which means it cannot be ignored and makes it worthy of attention in Chapter 8.

Because the curriculum is not taught to pupils who live in a vacuum, a number of complex factors impact upon individuals which transcend many areas of society, and these are explored in Chapter 9. Arguably the most significant of these are 'gender', 'social class' and 'race and ethnicity'. Sometimes described as the 'trinity' by those who study aspects of physical activity in society, they provide valuable lenses with which to examine and explain the decisions that we make.

Chapter 10 concerns itself with the transition between primary schools to secondary school which is a period of anxiety for many children. The significance of the transition from primary to secondary school in the UK and its global equivalent has been viewed as one of the most difficult in pupils' educational careers. Subjects such as Physical Education are not immune from such a transition and are an area of the curriculum which require particular attention given that pupils are exposed to significantly different environments, equipment and pedagogical approaches. Failure to give adequate attention here can undo much of the good work that may have been done to continue the development of a child's lifelong physical activity. Transition literature consistently uses the term 'bridges' as crucial links that must be negotiated as children move between primary and secondary schools and the concept is used here as useful tool to explain significant areas that should be understood within Physical Education.

What becomes clear from reading this text is that understanding primary Physical Education is a complex world of interrelationships. While it might be argued that because of such complexity its future would be difficult to predict, it is precisely because of this complexity that reasonable speculations can be made. By the use of ethnographic fiction, Chapter 11 creates possible scenarios that might occur and explores how these events might have unfolded.

KEY READINGS

As indicated here in the introduction, to get a broad overview of relevant issues pertaining to Physical Education, one needs to look no further than my previous text, Griggs, G. (ed.) (2012) *Physical Education in the Primary School: An Introduction* (London: Routledge). For broader issues within Physical Education, a good start would be the similarly titled Green, K. (2008) *Understanding Physical Education* (London: Sage). Beyond the very well established Physical Education journals such as *European Physical Education Review*, *Physical Education and Sport Pedagogy* and *Sport, Education and Society*, readers might wish to consider Physical Education related papers in wider spheres, in education or sociology journals such as *Education 3–13* or *Sociological Research Online*.

2

LOCATING PRIMARY PHYSICAL EDUCATION

Introduction

Many books examining Physical Education begin with chapters seeking to distil the essence of what is *meant* by Physical Education. For each of these books yet another definition is added to the pile and we are not arguably any the wiser in our understanding. In lay terms Capel and Whitehead (2012: 4) indicate that Physical Education simply 'means different things to different people'. This is perhaps unsurprising when one reads the work of Gallie (1968) and discovers that the nature of Physical Education meets the criteria for that of an essentially contested concept.

As Begley (1996: 403) explains:

> Essentially contested concepts are those that have no governing laws that define them, nor do they have agreed upon definitions of what they are about. Rather they tend to present themselves in 'schools of thought', 'ways of thinking', and so on ... thus with essentially contested concepts, we need to decide whose case is stronger, which side we believe in, and where we stand. We need, in fact, to be seduced by the texts and narratives.

If we are therefore to comprehend *where* we and others currently stand and perhaps more importantly *why*, it is important to understand the key texts and narratives that impact upon such stances. Across the world, most, if not all, of these are located within the fields of sport, education and health (Houlihan and Green, 2006; Penney, 2008). However from country to country and from era to era the dominance of one field compared to another can vary. The key explanation for this variation is that at any one time a culture becomes seduced by different texts and narratives and thus the power balance shifts resulting in what sociologists may call a hegemonic relationship (Gramsci, 1971). Attention will now turn to look at this complex and changing relationship that sport, education and health have with Physical Education in order to effectively locate it and furthermore how this relationship has impacted at primary school level particularly within the UK.

Physical Education and sport

Within UK movement culture as a whole, sport has occupied a dominant position for a large part of the twentieth century and beyond (Crum, 1993). Though McIntosh (1968) identifies a range of motives that sport has fulfilled over time such as aspects of playfulness, participation, enjoyment and catharsis, it has been the conception of sport as a highly competitive activity which has most characterised our notions of contemporary sport. In the UK, the main setting for the early development of contemporary sport was the boys' public schools, which focused largely upon organised team games. 'These games were infused with a Victorian version of masculinity, which celebrated competitiveness, toughness and physical dominance' (Theberge, 2000: 32). Thus the earliest direct influence upon Physical Education from sport was most keenly felt through the addition of these imported team games to the 'state' school curriculum in 1906 (McIntosh, 1976). During the twentieth century as men began to enter the teaching profession in larger numbers they championed a skills-focused approach, typical of sports and particularly team games (Kirk, 1992).

As a consequence, pedagogically, a skills-focused approach has been pervasive for generations within both coaching and teaching structures (Whitehead and Hendry, 1976). This mode of pedagogical practice of Physical Education as *sport techniques* has been created and continually regenerated (Kirk, 2011) suggesting perhaps the existence of an implicit agreement among school practitioners, particularly within secondary education, which has served to construct a Physical Education landscape dominated by a 'sporting model' (Capel, 2007: 494). In practice this has resulted in Physical Education continuing to be delivered using a limited range of teaching approaches, the most prevalent of which are formal, didactic and teacher centred (Green, 1998; Metzler, 2000; Kirk and Kinchin, 2003; Kirk, 2010). Over time the dominant discourse has shifted 'away from valuing individual creativity and problem solving towards performance, away from process to product' (Wright, 1996: 340). Subsequent curriculum designs over the last half a century continue to draw upon these ideas (Kirk, 2003) and this will be explored and illustrated further in Chapter 3.

What is worth noting here is that the Office for Standards in Education (OFSTED) reviews of Physical Education within primary schools over the last decade continually highlight recurring themes which indicate the influence of sport. In particular an over-concentration on performance and the delivery of an imbalanced curriculum dominated by games (see Office for Standards in Education, 1998; 2005; 2009). This dominant pedagogy has further been reinforced by the increased delivery of Physical Education by inexpensive non-QTS personnel, in particular sports coaches (Blair and Capel, 2011). Despite concerns raised in both OFSTED reports and research papers the significant input of these sport specialists has merely lent renewed vigour to the enduring 'sporting model', particularly at the primary school level (Capel, 2007; OFSTED, 2009). Furthermore, within primary schools, class teachers have placed misconceived value upon the narrow subject knowledge exhibited by these sport coaches and as a result have willingly relinquished their Physical Education lessons to them (Ward, 2011; Griggs, 2010). All too often the consequence of what occurs during primary Physical Education lessons is the delivery of a watered-down version of a secondary Physical Education programme. For many children, however, these experiences are inappropriate, as the activities are too complex in relation to their current developmental status (Jess, 2011). Further explanation concerning the employment of external personnel and issues concerning teacher training and continuing professional development can be found in Chapters 4 and 5.

Physical Education and education

The marginalisation of Physical Education within school curricula is deeply rooted in philosophical thought in which the physical is considered subordinate to the mental. Such Cartesian perspectives on a mind–body split continue to pervade Western European approaches to education in which the physical remains separate and inferior to cognitive activity (Sparkes, Templin and Schempp, 1990). The writings of liberal analytical philosophers such as Richard Peters and Paul Hirst have done much to reinforce this position within mainstream education in the English-speaking world (Green, 2008). What is commonly known as the Peters–Hirst approach was based on the premise that education is concerned with valuable knowledge and that this knowledge was theoretical in nature and was concerned principally with the development of intelligence (Peters and Hirst, 1970). Being labelled as practical knowledge, the denunciation of physical activities contained within Physical Education were reduced to experiences in which pupils were merely required to learn a 'knack' or 'trick' (Peters, 1996). The hegemony of their 1970 thesis did much to propel Physical Education to a peripheral position, compared to subjects that are deeply rooted within rational forms of knowledge, such as Science and Mathematics.

McNamee (2005) indicates that this left Physical Educationalists with split paths to follow in which their subject would remain exclusively practical and thus marginal or become more academic and move towards containing valuable knowledge. The proliferation of GCSE and A level courses available in Physical Education in secondary education and the university courses concerning various aspects of sport, Physical Education and Physical Education teacher training, reflects the shift that has occurred to make these areas worthy of valuable academic study (Kirk, 2010). However schools and universities which seek to promote themselves upon academic excellence may well not continue to offer Physical Education as a mode of study. This position continues to be exemplified in primary schools.

In UK primary schools over the last decade there has been a heightened awareness of a results and an outcomes driven system, as measurable performance has been given greater value (Ball, 2003) to the point where performativity can be seen to be 'hijacking the creativity discourse' (Turner-Bisset, 2007: 201). In broad terms this has led to teachers delivering a narrow focus within any given programme of study (Compton, 2007) as 'most head teachers and subject leaders have concentrated on the raising standards agenda' (OFSTED, 2005: 2)

Nowhere has this impact been more sharply felt than in subjects such as Physical Education which have become increasingly marginalised within curriculum time, as a greater emphasis has been placed upon the teaching of core subjects such as English (Literacy), Mathematics (Numeracy) and Science for which annual results are published for all primary schools (Speednet, 2000; Warburton, 2001; OFSTED, 2005). Within such an environment, Physical Education for some has been reduced to something of a second-class subject (Griggs, 2007), taught at the end of a school day or as a break from focused, class-based learning and, as a consequence, there remains low expectations of primary Physical Education (OFSTED, 2005, 2009; Griggs, 2012).

THOUGHT BOX

Reflect on the place of primary Physical Education in a primary school that you are familiar with? What level of importance is given to it?

Physical Education and health

The hegemony of health within discourses of Physical Education in the UK predominated in the late nineteenth and early twentieth centuries. Indeed the associations between health and Physical Education in the UK can be traced to before the development of the Foster Act (1870), providing an education for all. From the 1850s onwards, the health benefits of Physical Education were framed in general and largely functional terms (Kirk, 1992). In this period, exercise was viewed as one of four elements contributing to health, along with nutrition, sanitary conditions and clean air (Thomson, 1979). The establishment of the first national syllabus however was quick to highlight the association between being physically active and healthy. Indeed, as early as 1905 the syllabus for 'Physical Training' explained that: 'The primary objective of any course of physical exercises in schools is to maintain, and if possible, improve the health and physique of the children' (Board of Education, 1905: 9). Subsequent revisions, such as the 1909 syllabus, further reinforced and detailed this objective

(Kirk, 1988) specifying key benefits of being physical through physical training, namely benefits to general health through efficient functioning of the body, remedial benefits such as correcting poor posture, and developmental benefits in terms of assisting the natural pattern of growth of the child (Dunlop, 1936).

A particular focus upon the capability to move efficiently became central to the development of the later 1933 syllabus and by this time, this was rooted explicitly in the notion of good posture (Tinning, 2001). The reason for such a focus came from the directive of the medical profession, whose association with Physical Education was closely aligned, illustrated by the fact that there was even a Physical Education committee of the BMA (Welshman, 1996). However following the Second World War the influence of exercise and health upon schooling were soon overtaken by a newfound interest in wider scientific study in which sport was located (McIntosh, 1968).

It was not until the 1980s that major discourses related to Physical Education began to return to physical health, although now health was to be viewed more holistically and included additional psychological aspects (Fox and Biddle, 1988). Within school curricula, piecemeal efforts of what were termed 'health-related exercise/activity/fitness' began to emerge (Cale and Harris, 2005). However, 'it was not until the mid-1990s that a number of key events moved matters forward. The main catalyst was a series of robust, longitudinal studies that identified the importance of regular physical activity across the lifespan' (Bailey et al., 2009: 7). From this point onwards engagement in physical activity emerged as an important public health issue and has remained in the political spotlight, most successfully in Scotland (HEA 1998; Scottish Executive, 2003). A draft primary curriculum in England also demonstrated a shift in thinking as Physical Education become located with an area titled 'Understanding Physical Development, Health and Well Being' (DCSF, 2009). However with a change in government in 2010 this draft was discarded. Following a political need to link primary Physical Education to the Olympic legacy of the London 2012 games, the new iteration of the NCPE maintained the hegemonic position of sport (see Chapter 3 for a fuller explanation on this topic).

Perhaps most pertinently rhetoric and research concerning health and primary Physical Education have continued to focus attention upon physical inactivity and links with childhood obesity (Steinbeck, 2001). However, close examination reveals that much of the evidence is less than compelling (Biddle et al., 2004). An important outcome of increased attention on physical activity/ inactivity was the development of age-appropriate national physical activity guidelines for children, recommending the accumulation of at least one hour of physical activity per day (NASPE 1995, 2002; HEA, 1998). The sustained impact of this guidance on school Physical Education programmes appears to be, as yet, limited (Cale and Harris, 2005). That said, significant authors in the field such as Trost (2006: 183) still maintain that, 'school physical education programs are uniquely situated to address the epidemic of obesity and sedentary behaviour plaguing our youth worldwide'. With health agendas becoming centred towards performance outcomes, with the emergence of performative health and a proliferation of policies geared towards measuring and defining young people's bodies (Evans et al., 2008), health could well become reduced to yet another measurable outcome for which teachers and schools are to be responsible. Indeed Tinning (2012) indicates that renewed focus upon linking health and Physical Education could well dominate the next texts and narratives that we may well be seduced by.

Physical Education within UK movement culture: a significant disconnection

Clearly areas such as education, sport and health have served as powerful attractors that have influenced and shaped what Physical Education has become over time. Though issues of commonality may be found across the world it is the movement culture within which Physical Education is located that serves to highlight useful areas for critical discussion (Crum, 1993).

Movement culture is in essence 'an umbrella concept which comprises all leisure actions in which the human moving act is the essence' (Crum, 1994: 115). A common term within German and Dutch languages, seeking to avoid mind–body dualisms, it more specifically 'refers to the way in which a social group deals with the need and desire for movement beyond labour or maintaining life. Movement culture contains the set of movement actions and interactions (sport, play, dance, or other fitness activities) that encompass a group's leisure' (Crum, 1993: 341). Movement cultures are of course incredibly diverse and reflective of different times and spaces.

One need only compare traditional dances and related costumes and music from across the world to quickly illustrate such a concept. In addition it is important to note that as with any concept of culture it is also susceptible to change and influence. Illustrative of this point are a culture's changing habits of food consumption. What we ate a century ago will contrast markedly with our diets and choices of today, the purpose of which extends beyond the sole need for survival. Crum (1994: 118) indicates that within recent times, the broader cultural landscape and 'the movement-cultural landscape has drastically changed'. By contrast there is considerable evidence to suggest that Physical Education has not, creating a significant disconnection (Griggs and Ward, 2012).

Beck (2011) explains this broad cultural shift in Westernised countries as a move from first modernity to that of second modernity. From this perspective, in first modernity social relations operate within a contained area – for example, on a national, regional and local level. Furthermore, most institutions are closely related to the nation-state. The freedom and equality of its individuals are moulded by powerful social institutions to which they are strongly adhered and disciplined by, such as the workplace (factories and unions), school and the Church (Beck et al., 2003). By contrast, in second modernity, society is far more globalised and borderless which has been facilitated by developments in technology. Changes in family, working practices and roles have also occurred, most notably a shift towards egalitarian viewpoints on gender (Beck and Beck-Gernsheim, 1995). In addition a more intense political individualisation has developed a consumerist and choice-driven society which sees less legitimacy in traditional social institutions (Beck and Beck-Gernsheim, 2001). Beck (2011: 281) concludes this leaves us with 'a new kind of society and a new kind of personal life [that] are coming into being'. In this new society, traditional collective organisations such as the Church, labour unions, family and school command less power than they once did (Giddens, 1991). Rather than choosing to be seen to have prescribed or standard identities through memberships and affiliations there is an unabated trend towards people coming to think of themselves as unique individuals, exercising self-consciousness, creativity and agency (Prout, 2000). Among young people, Beck (1998: 78) suggests that within Western cultures this concept of individualisation is so strong that they 'no longer become individualized. They individualize themselves. The "biographization" of youth means becoming active, struggling and designing one's own life.' (Beck, 1998: 78). The traditional values espoused by dominant sporting forms and traditional Physical Education practice represent the antithesis of this viewpoint (Griggs and Ward, 2012). Holland and Thomson (1999) indicate that the prevailing attitude on the part of young people in empirical findings thrives in new kinds of institutions in which authority, and allegiance, must be constantly renegotiated, re-established and earned. In short, in an increasingly individualised world, young people articulate an 'ethic of reciprocity arguing that their respect could be won by anyone who respected them ... they tend to be very wary of claims to authority and respect on the basis of tradition, custom or force' (Prout, 2000: 308).

As it stands, Physical Education currently taught in UK schools increasingly fails to engage young people and thus fails to prepare them to become active creators and consumers of the varied forms of physical activity available outside school (Sandford and Rich, 2006; Griggs and Ward, 2012). What has sadly resulted, at a time when obesity rates are rising and populations are becoming increasingly sedentary (Fairclough and Stratton, 1997; Green, 2002; Basterfield et al., 2011), is the alienation of a significant number of those young people

---

THOUGHT BOX

It is important for those who like and enjoy Physical Education to empathise with the clear majority of people who do not. Recognising that most of the population in the UK drop out of or drop off their relationship with physical activity, what ideas might you have for making it appealing to the masses? Working backwards, what needs to be done with primary-aged pupils to ensure those ideas can develop successfully?

(Green, 2012; Kirk and Macdonald, 1998). Low participation in a physically active, healthy lifestyle is a major concern, exacerbated by the cycle of reproduction of practice within Physical Education. This process has proven to be enduring and surprisingly resistant to change (Alfrey et al., 2012; Capel, 2007; Tsangaridou, 2006). As such the potential for further dissatisfaction and disengagement from Physical Education remains extremely high (Griggs and Stidder, 2012).

Conclusion

Perhaps the most obvious way forward to reconnect Physical Education within UK movement culture is to embrace Crum's (1994: 116) proposal that 'Physical Education should be arranged in view of learning with utility value for the movement culture outside the school [maximising] its potential to qualify youngsters for an emancipated, satisfying and lasting participation'. The viewpoint of emancipation for young people has a resonance with the ideals of second modernity and could be embraced rather than resisted. This might, therefore, include a movement culture which allows children opportunities such as learning to swim and ride a bike, but also supports their progress through a multitude of activities and experiences they need in later life. Crum (1993) considers that the activities children need to be prepared for to support their active participation within the wider movement culture may need to include: elite sport, competitive club sport, recreation sport, fitness sport, risk and adventure, lust sport and cosmetic sport. Though this and other classifications may be debated, what is clear is a need to make Physical Education relevant to more young people and reconnect it to the wider movement culture. To achieve this reconnection its position needs to be more reflective of the era of second modernity as opposed to the era of first modernity in which it was conceived.

The difficulty that faces Physical Education researchers and practitioners here is that to date there remains little empirical evidence that Physical Education can claim to have had a direct or specific effect (termed by Green (2012: 1) as the 'PE effect') on a individual's future of physical activity. The extensive review of Physical Education literature conducted Bailey et al. (2009) concurs, identifying that much is claimed but little can be proven. Perhaps the best we are left with is that active participation in different forms of physical activity during childhood and youth 'is an important prerequisite for involvement in later life' (Green, 2012: 18). If the basic foundations of lifelong physical activity are therefore laid during the primary-aged years (see Birchwood et al., 2008; Scheerder et al., 2006) what needs to be ensured is that children become both competent and confident in a range of relevant activities in a range of different environments (Griggs and Stidder, 2012). As can be seen in Chapter 3, the challenge is to decide which activities should be chosen and what is deemed as relevant to be selected for inclusion into a Physical Education curriculum.

KEY READINGS

Locating primary Physical Education within a nexus of sport, education and health is a useful exercise enabling its relevance and purpose to be considered. A useful paper exploring the issues raised in this chapter still further is Griggs, G. and Ward, G. (2012) Physical Education in the UK: disconnections and reconnections, *Curriculum Journal*, 23(2), 207–229. The beliefs and claims that Physical Education have significant and positive effects on young people are many and varied but may not in fact be well substantiated. For a full review of the Physical Education literature see Bailey, R., Armour, K., Kirk, D., Jess, M., Pickup, I., Sandford, R. and BERA Physical Education and Sport Pedagogy Special Interest Group (2009), The educational benefits claimed for Physical Education and school sport: an academic review, *Research Papers in Education*, 24(1), 1–27.

References

Alfrey, L., Cale, L. and Webb, L. (2012) Physical Education teachers' continuing professional development in health-related exercise, *Physical Education and Sport Pedagogy*, 17(5), 477–491.

Bailey, R., Armour, K., Kirk, D., Jess, M., Pickup, I., Sandford, R. and BERA Physical Education and Sport Pedagogy Special Interest Group (2009) The educational benefits claimed for physical education and school sport: an academic review, *Research Papers in Education*, 24(1), 1–27.

Ball, S.J. (2003) The teacher's soul and the terrors of performativity, *Journal of Education Policy*, 18(2), 215–228.

Basterfield, L., Adamson, A.J., Frary, J.K., Parkinson, K.N., Pearce, M.S. and Reilly, J.J. (2011) Longitudinal study of physical activity and sedentary behaviour in children, *Pediatrics*, 127(1), e24–e30.

Beck, U. (1998) *Democracy Without Enemies*. Cambridge: Polity Press.

Beck, U. (2011) The Cosmopolitan Manifesto. In D. Held and G. Brown (eds) *The Cosmopolitanism Reader*. Cambridge: Polity Press.

Beck, U. and Beck-Gernsheim, E. (1995) *The Normal Chaos of Love*. Cambridge: Polity Press.

Beck, U. and Beck-Gernsheim, E. (2001) *Individualization*. London: Sage.

Beck, U., Bonss, W. and Lau, C. (2003) The Theory of Reflexive Modernization: Problematic, Hypotheses and Research Programme, *Theory Culture Society*, 20(2), 1–33.

Begley, P.T. (1996) Cognitive perspectives on values in administration: A quest for coherence and relevance, *Educational Administration Quarterly*, 32(3), 403–426.

Biddle, S.J.H., Gorely, T. and Stensel, D. (2004) Health-enhancing physical activity and sedentary behaviour in children and adolescents, *Journal of Sports Sciences*, 22, 679–701.

Birchwood, D., Roberts, K. and Pollock, G. (2008) Explaining differences in sport participation rates among young adults: evidence from the South Caucasus, *European Physical Education Review*, 14(3), 283–300.

Blair, R. and Capel, S. (2011) Primary physical education, coaches and continuing professional development, *Sport, Education and Society*, 16(4), 485–505.

Board of Education (1905) *Syllabus of Physical Exercises for Public Elementary Schools.* London: HMSO.

Cale, L.A. and Harris, J. (eds) (2005) *Exercise and Young People: Issues, Implications and Initiative.* Basingstoke: Palgrave Macmillan.

Capel, S. (2007) Moving beyond physical education subject knowledge to develop knowledgeable teachers of the subject, *Curriculum Journal*, 18(4), 493–507.

Capel, S. and Whitehead, M. (2012) What is Physical Education? In S. Capel and M. Whitehead (eds) *Debates in Physical Education.* London: Routledge.

Compton, A. (2007) Bringing creativity back into primary education, *Education 3–13*, 35(2), 109–116.

Crum, B. (1993) Conventional thought and practice in Physical Education: problems of teaching and implications for change, *Quest*, 45, 339–356.

Crum, B. (1994) Changes in movement culture: challenges for sport pedagogy. Proceedings from the AISEP conference, 2, Sport Leisure and Physical Education, Trends and Developments.

Department for Children, Schools and Families (DCSF) (2009) *Independent Review of the Primary Curriculum: Final Report.* London: DCSF.

Dunlop, J.L. (1936) The development of physical training for school children and adolescents, *The Journal of the Royal Society for the Promotion of Health*, 57, 787–794.

Evans, J., Rich, E. and Davies, B. (2008) How not to approach weight management in schools. The damaging effects of health education in totally pedagogised 'healthy' schools, *Physical Education Matters*, 3(1), 28–33.

Fairclough, S. and Stratton, G. (1997) PE curriculum and extra curriculum time in schools in the north-west of England, *British Journal of Physical Education*, 28(3), 21–24.

Fox, K. and Biddle, S. (1988) The child's perspective in physical education part 2: children's participation motives, *British Journal of Physical Education*, 19(2), 17–82.

Gallie, W.B. (1968) *Philosophy and the Historical Understanding.* New York: Schocken Books.

Giddens, A. (1991) *Modernity and Self-identity. Self and Society in the Late Modern Age.* Oxford: Polity Press.

Gramsci, A. (1971) *Selections from the Prison Notebooks of Antonio Gramsci.* G. Nowell-Smith and Q. Hoare (eds) New York: International Publishers.

Green, K. (1998) Philosophies, ideologies and the practice of physical education, *Sport, Education and Society*, 3, 125–143.

Green, K. (2002) Physical Education and the 'couch potato society': part one, *Physical Education and Sport Pedagogy*, 7(2), 95–107.

Green, K. (2008) *Understanding Physical Education.* London: Sage.

Green, K. (2012) Mission impossible? Reflecting upon the relationship between physical education, youth sport and lifelong participation, *Sport, Education and Society* (ahead of print), 1–19.

Griggs, G. (2007) Physical Education: primary matters, secondary importance, *Education 3–13*, 35(1), 59–69.

Griggs, G. (2010) For sale – primary Physical Education. £20 per hour or nearest offer, *Education 3–13*, 38(1), 39–46.

Griggs, G. (2012) Introduction – surveying the landscape. In G. Griggs (ed.) (2012) *Physical Education in the Primary School: An Introduction.* London: Routledge.

Griggs, G. and Stidder, G. (2012) Healthism and the obesity discourse: approaches to inclusive health education through alternative Physical Education. In G. Stidder and S. Hayes (eds) *Equity and Inclusion in Physical Education* (2nd edition). London: Routledge.

Griggs, G. and Ward, G. (2012) Physical Education in the UK: disconnections and reconnections, *Curriculum Journal*, 23(2), 207–229.

Health Education Authority (HEA) (1998) *Young and Active? Policy Framework for Young People and Health-enhancing Physical Activity.* London: Health Education Authority.

Holland, J. and Thomson, R. (1999) Respect – youth values: identity, diversity and social change, ESRC Children 5–16 Research Programme Briefing. London: ESRC.

Houlihan, B. and Green, M. (2006) The changing status of school sport and physical education: explaining policy change, *Sport, Education and Society*, 11(1), 73–92.

Jess, M. (2011) Becoming an effective primary school teacher. In K. Armour (ed.) *Sport Pedagogy*. Harlow: Prentice Hall.

Kirk, D. (1988) *Physical Education and Curriculum Study: A Critical Introduction*. Beckenham: Croome Helm.

Kirk, D. (1992) *Defining Physical Education: The Social Construction of a School Subject in Post-war Britain*. London: Falmer.

Kirk, D. (2003) Sport, Physical Education and schools. In B. Houlihan (ed.) *Sport in Society*. London: Sage.

Kirk, D. (2010) *Physical Education Futures*. London: Routledge.

Kirk, D. (2011) The crisis of content knowledge: How PETE maintains the id? of physical education-as-sport-techniques (part 3), *Physical Education Matters*, 6(2), 34–36.

Kirk, D. and Kinchin, G. (2003) Situated learning as a theoretical framework for sport education, *European Physical Education Review*, 9(3), 221–236.

Kirk, D. and Macdonald, D. (1998) Situated learning in physical education, *Journal of Teaching in Physical Education*, 17, 376–387.

McIntosh, P.C. (1968) *Physical Education in England Since 1800*. London: Bell.

McIntosh, P. (1976) The curriculum of physical education – an historical perspective. In J. Kane (ed.) *Curriculum Development in Physical Education*. London: Crosby Lockwood Staples.

McNamee, M. (2005) The nature and values of Physical Education. In K. Green and K. Hardman (eds) *Physical Education: Essential Issues* (pp. 1–20). London: Sage.

Metzler, M. (ed.) (2000) The physical education teacher education assessment project, *Journal of Teaching in Physical Education* (special edition), 19(4), 293–309.

National Association for Physical Education (NASPE) (1995) *Moving into the Future: National Physical Education Standards: A Guide to Content and Assessment*. St Louis, MI: Mosby.

National Association for Physical Education (NASPE) (2002) *Active Start. A Statement of Physical Activity Guidelines for Children, Birth to Five Years*. Reston, VA: NASPE.

Office for Standards in Education (Ofsted) (1998) *Teaching Physical Education in the Primary School: The Initial Training of Teachers*. London: HMSO.

Office for Standards in Education (Ofsted) (2005) *Physical Education in Primary Schools*. London: TSO.

Office for Standards in Education (Ofsted) (2009) *Physical Education in Primary Schools (2005–2008)*. London: TSO.

Penney, D. (2008) Playing a political game and play for position: policy and curriculum development in health and PE, *European PE Review*, 4(1), 33–49.

Peters, R.S. (1996) *Ethics and Education*. London: Allen and Unwin.

Peters, R.S. and Hirst, P. (1970) *The Logic of Education*. London: Routledge and Kegan Paul.

Prout, A. (2000) Children's participation: control and self-realisation in British late modernity, *Children and Society*, 14, 304–315.

Sandford, R. and Rich, E. (2006) Learners and popular culture. In D. Kirk, D. Macdonald and M. O'Sullivan (eds) *The Handbook of Physical Education*. London: Sage.

Scheerder, J., Thomis, M., Vanreusel, B., Lefevre, J., Renson, R., Vanden Eynde, B. and Beunen, G.P. (2006) Sports participation among females from adolescence to adulthood, *International Review for the Sociology of Sport*, 41(3–4), 413–430.

Scottish Executive (2003) *Let's Make Scotland More Active: A Strategy for Physical Activity.* Edinburgh: HMSO.

Sparkes, A., Templin, T. and Schempp, P. (1990) The problematic nature of a career in a marginal subject: some implications for teacher education, *Journal of Education for Teaching*, 16(1), 3–28.

Speednet (2000) Primary school physical education – Speednet survey makes depressing reading, *British Journal of Physical Education*, 30(3), 19–20.

Steinbeck, K.S. (2001) The importance of physical activity in the prevention of overweight and obesity in childhood: a review and an opinion, *Obesity Reviews*, 2, 117–130.

Theberge, N. (2000) Gender and Sport. In J. Coakley and E. Dunning (eds) *Handbook of Sports Studies*. London: Sage.

Thomson, I. (1979) Over-pressure and physical deterioration factors leading to the acceptance of Physical Education 1880–1895, *Physical Education Review*, 2(2), 115–122.

Tinning, R. (2001) Physical Education and back health: negotiating instrumental aims and holistic bodywork practices, *European Physical Education Review*, 7(2), 191–205.

Tinning, R. (2012) The idea of physical education: a memetic perspective, *Physical Education and Sport Pedagogy*, 17(2), 115–126.

Turner-Bissett, R. (2007) Performativity by stealth: a critique of recent initiatives on creativity, *Education 3–13*, 35(2), 193–203.

Trost, S. (2006) Public health and physical education. In D. Kirk, D. Macdonald and M. O'Sullivan (eds) *The Handbook of Physical Education*. London: Sage.

Tsangaridou, N. (2006) Teachers' beliefs. In Kirk, D., Macdonald, D. and O'Sullivan, M. (eds) *The Handbook of Physical Education*. London: Sage.

Warburton, P. (2001) A sporting future for all: fact or fiction, *The British Journal of Teaching Physical Education*, 32(2), 18–21.

Ward, G. (2011) Examining primary school Physical Education coordinators' pedagogical content knowledge of games: simply playing?, *Education 3–13*, 41(6), 562–585.

Welshman, J. (1996) Physical Education and the School Medical Service in England and Wales 1907–1939, *Social History of Medicine*, 9(1), 31–48.

Whitehead, N. and Hendry, L. (1976) *Teaching Physical Education in England – Description and Analysis*. London: Lepus.

Wright, J. (1996) Mapping the discourses of physical education: articulating a female tradition, *Journal of Curriculum Studies*, 28(3), 331–351.

3

PHYSICAL EDUCATION IN THE PRIMARY CURRICULUM

Introduction

Historically, the story of primary education within the United Kingdom has been comparatively short. It was not until the 1960s that pupils aged five to eleven could be educated in schools specifically designed for that age range (Oliver, 2004). Yet by the end of the decade, two seminal but polarising documents – namely, the Plowden Report (CACE, 1967) and the 'Black Papers' (Cox and Dyson, 1969a, 1969b) – would represent key viewpoints on what would quickly become highly contested terrain. The Plowden Report encapsulated child-centred theories of education enshrined in its maxim 'at the heart of education lies the child'. It was unashamedly humanistic in tone and brought the needs of children to the fore by encouraging them 'to be themselves and to develop in the way and at the pace appropriate to them' (CACE, 1967: 187). In practical terms, the report paved the way for the expansion of nursery education, the greater involvement of parents and gave schools the freedom to determine their own curriculum ideas (Oliver, 2004). In stark contrast the polemic 'Black Papers' (so-called in direct opposition to Government White Papers) spelt out a distinct conservative and traditional vision of education, positioning themselves against so called 'progressive', 'liberal' ideas purveyed in the Plowden Report and championing a subject focused, teacher directed and prescribed curriculum (Harnett and Vinney, 2008). Finding a balance between these opposing viewpoints coloured the educational landscape for the next two decades and prompted the HMI publication of a series of documents which summarised key aspects of the debate. In 'The Curriculum from 5–16', HMI stressed the importance of a holistic view of education, with the necessity of locating core educational experiences within broad areas of learning (DES, 1985). This thinking shaped the drafting of the Education Reform Act (ERA, 1988), which led to the first incarnation of the national curriculum in England and Wales.

THOUGHT BOX

Try starting with a blank piece of paper and decide what should be in a national curriculum for primary Physical Education. Consider what activities might or might not be included and what learning should occur.

Physical Education within the national curriculum in England and Wales

Despite the holistic vision advocated by HMI, the Education Reform Act specified the need for a focus on separate subjects. English, Maths and Science were determined to be *core* to the new curriculum, whilst another six areas, of which Physical Education was one, where termed *foundation* subjects (DES, 1991). The content, or 'Programme of Study', of each subject was then created by separate working groups. However, 'since the subject groups worked largely in isolation from each other, when the programmes of study for each subject were published there was little evidence of an integrated vision for children's learning experiences and how links between different subjects may be developed' (Harnett and Vinney, 2008: 123). Within primary Physical Education, pupils were required to experience six activity areas: athletic activities, dance, games, gymnastic activities, outdoor and adventurous activities, and swimming. The requirements for these were divided into Key Stages 1 and 2, arbitrary lines drawn at seven and eleven years of age respectively, with 'End of Key Stage Statements' expressing idealised pupil attainment (DES, 1991). (See Boxes 3.1 to 3.3 below.)

Though the newly formed curriculum gave primary pupils significantly more breadth in most cases, fitting all the prescribed content for all subjects into a school timetable soon became a concern (Campbell and Neill, 1992; Webb, 1993) and to avoid omissions, schools were urged to plan extremely

---

BOX 3.1 NATIONAL CURRICULUM FOR PHYSICAL EDUCATION 1991 – KEY STAGE 1 (DES, 1991)

Programme of study for Key Stage 1

Athletic activities

Pupils should:

- experience and be encouraged to take part in running, jumping and throwing activities, concentrating on accuracy, speed, height, length and distance.

Dance

Pupils should:

- experience and develop control, co-ordination, balance, poise and elevation in basic actions including travelling, gesture and stillness;
- work on contrasts of speed, tension, continuity, shape, size, direction and level;
- experience working with a range, and contrasting stimuli, including music;
- be helped to develop rhythmic responses;
- be given opportunities to explore moods and feelings through spontaneous responses;
- through structured tasks, experience and be guided towards making dances with clear beginnings, middles and ends.

Games

Pupils should:

- experience using a variety of games equipment, such as balls and implements of different weights and sizes;
- experience, practice and develop a variety of ways of sending, receiving and travelling with a ball;
- experience elements of games play that include chasing, dodging, avoiding and awareness of space and other players;
- be given opportunities to make up and play games with simple rules and objectives that include one person and a limited amount of equipment.

Gymnastic activities

Pupils should:

- experience many ways of performing the basic actions of travelling, turning, rolling, jumping, balancing, swinging, climbing and taking weight on hands, both on the floor and using apparatus;
- be given opportunities to practise, adapt and improve their control of individual actions;
- be given opportunities to link together a series of actions both on the floor and using apparatus, and be able to repeat them;
- be taught to carry and position simple apparatus, including the correct lifting technique.

Outdoor and adventurous activities

Pupils should:

- explore the potential for physical activities within the immediate environment;

- undertake simple orientation activities;
- apply physical skills out of doors on climbing frames or other playground equipment.

Swimming

Where swimming is taught in Key Stage 1, pupils should follow the programme of study set out in Key Stage 2. Where pupils do not start swimming lessons until part way through Key Stage 1, they should be taught only part of the programme of study.

(DES, 1991)

BOX 3.2 NATIONAL CURRICULUM FOR PHYSICAL EDUCATION 1991 – KEY STAGE 2 (DES, 1991)

Programme of study for Key Stage 2

Athletic activities

Pupils should:
- practise and develop basic actions in running (over short and longer distances and in relays), throwing and jumping;
- be given opportunities for and guidance in measuring, comparing and improving their own performance;
- experience completions, including those they make up themselves.

Dance

Pupils should, individually, with a partner and in small groups:
- be guided to enrich their movements by varying shape, size, direction, level, speed, tension and continuity;
- be given opportunities to increase the range and complexity of body actions, including step patterns and turning while travelling;
- make dances with clear beginnings, middles and ends involving improvising/exploring, selecting and refining content and sometimes incorporating work from other aspects of the curriculum, in particular music and art;
- in response to a range of stimuli, express feelings, moods and ideas, and create simple characters and narratives in movement.

Games

Pupils should, individually, with a partner and in small groups:
* explore and be guided to an understanding of the common skills and principles, including attack and defence, in invasion, net/wall and striking/fielding games;
* be helped to improve the skills of sending, receiving and travelling with a ball for invasion, net/wall and striking/fielding games;
* be given opportunities to develop their own games practices, working towards objectives decided sometimes by themselves and sometimes by the teacher;
* make up, play and refine their own games within prescribed limits, considering and developing rules and scoring systems;
* develop an understanding of and play games created by the teacher as well as small sided, simplified versions of recognised games covering invasion, net/wall and striking/fielding games.

Gymnastic activities

Pupils should:
* be enabled, both on the floor and using apparatus, to find more ways of rolling, jumping, swinging, balancing and taking weight on hands and to adapt, practise and refine these actions;
* be guided to perform in a controlled manner and to understand that the ending of one action can become the beginning of the next;
* be enabled and given opportunities to respond to a variety of tasks emphasising such things as changing shape, speed and direction through gymnastic actions;
* be given opportunities, both on the floor and using apparatus in response to set tasks, explore, select, develop, practise and refine a longer series of actions making increasingly complex movement sequences which they are able to repeat.

Outdoor and adventurous activities

Pupils should:
* learn the principles of safety in the outdoors and develop the ability to assess and respond to possible hazards in a variety of contexts and conditions and how to avoid danger;
* experience in the course of the key stage, at least one exciting and challenging activity in an unfamiliar environment;
* be taught the skills necessary for the activity undertaken and how to avoid danger and minimise risk, including the correct use of appropriate equipment.

Swimming

Pupils should:

- learn the principles of water safety, to assess the nature, visibility and location of water hazards in a variety of conditions and how to avoid danger;
- be taught water safety and survival skills appropriate to their competence in water and to evaluate their own abilities and limitations relative to safety in a variety of conditions;
- be made aware of the role of swimming and water safety skills in supporting other water based activities and activities near water;
- be given opportunities to develop confidence in water, learn how to rest in water and which floating and support positions and methods of propulsion are most appropriate for a variety of situations;
- experience and understand the relationships between flotation and body alignment and position, breathing, clothing, etc.;
- learn a variety of means of propulsion using either arms or legs or both, and develop effective and efficient swimming strokes on front and back;
- be given opportunities to work in pairs and in groups to assess situations in personal survival and life saving, adopt appropriate courses of action and evaluate the results;
- be encouraged to test their swimming and water skills efficiency against a range of criteria;
- learn the codes of hygiene and courtesy for using public swimming pools.

(DES, 1991)

BOX 3.3 NATIONAL CURRICULUM FOR PHYSICAL EDUCATION 1991 – STATEMENTS OF ATTAINMENT – LEVELS 1–4 (DES, 1991)

Pupils should be able to:

Level 1

- perform simple movements with and without equipment with confidence and control;
- respond safely to a simple task in a variety of ways;
- use movement to show moods and feelings and respond to simple rhythms and contrasting stimuli;
- recognise and describe in simple terms changes that happen to their bodies during activity.

Level 2

- link movements, to show increasing control in changing directions and levels, appropriate use of energy and power and moving rhythmically;
- practise and perform simple games skills;
- make up and adapt simple games skills they play on their own to improve basic skills;
- recognise, explain and work within rules;
- describe what they and others have done using functional and aesthetic terms;
- recognise and abide by safety requirements in different environments, including moving and using equipment.

Level 3

- plan and perform sequences of movement alone and with others;
- improve performance through practice and rehearsal;
- play simple games with others, including those they make up and those initiated by the teacher;
- plan, use and judge the success of simple tactics;
- make simple judgements of how others have performed movements;
- experience and understand at a basic level the short term effects of exercise on the body.

Level 4

- explore and present different responses to a variety of stimuli tasks;
- refine and adapt performance when working with others;
- repeat series of movements they have remembered after a period of time;
- understand and apply simple concepts of attack and defence in games;
- swim a minimum distance of 25 metres and be safe in and around water, knowing their limitations;
- make simple judgements of their own and others performance using aesthetic and functional criteria;
- understand and demonstrate how to prepare themselves and recover from particular activities;
- understand the value of and demonstrate sustained activity.

(DES, 1991)

carefully (Ofsted, 1993). These difficulties prompted the Dearing Review, which found that the initial orders were unworkable, expressing that, 'the architects of the first subject curricula designed what for them, as subject specialists for the most part, was an ideal and comprehensive curriculum for each subject. Not until this was put into practice in classrooms did it become obvious that the combined weight of all the subject curricula was simply too great to be manageable' (SCAA, 1994: 1).

A further revision of the National Curriculum was produced in light of this review which largely saw the breadth of curriculum maintained but the prescribed content within each subject significantly reduced (Rawling, 2001). (See Boxes 3.4 to 3.6.)

BOX 3.4 NATIONAL CURRICULUM FOR PHYSICAL EDUCATION 1995 – KEY STAGE 1 (DFES, 1995)

General requirements for Key Stage 1

1. To promote physical activity and healthy lifestyles:
    a. to be physically active;
    b. to adopt the best possible posture and the appropriate use of the body;
    c. to engage in activities that develop cardiovascular health, flexibility, muscular strength and endurance.
2. To develop positive attitudes, pupils should be taught:
    a. to observe the conventions of fair play, honest competition and good sporting behaviour as individual participants, team members and spectators;
    b. how to cope with success and limitations in performance;
    c. to try hard to consolidate their performance;
    d. to be mindful of others and the environment.
3. To ensure safe practice, pupils should be taught:
    a. to respond readily to instructions;
    b. to recognise and follow relevant rules, laws, codes and etiquette and safety procedures for different activities or events, in practice and during competition;
    c. about the safety risks of wearing inappropriate clothing, footwear and jewellery and why particular clothing, footwear and protection are worn for different activities;
    d. how to lift, carry, place and use equipment safely;
    e. to warm up for and recover from exercise.

Key Stage 1

Areas of activity

Games

Pupils should be taught:

a.   simple competitive games, including how to play them as individuals and, when ready, in pairs and in small groups;

b.   to develop and practise a variety of ways of sending (including throwing, striking, rolling and bouncing), receiving and travelling with a ball and other similar games equipment;

c.   elements of games play that include running, chasing, dodging, avoiding and awareness of space and other players.

Gymnastic activities

a.   different ways of performing the basic actions of travelling using hands and feet, turning, rolling, jumping, balancing, swinging and climbing, both on the floor and using apparatus;

b.   to link a series of actions both on the floor and using apparatus, and how to repeat them.

Dance

a.   to develop control, co-ordination, balance, poise and elevation to the basic actions of travelling, jumping, turning, gesture and stillness;

b.   to perform movements or patterns, including some from existing dance traditions;

c.   to explore moods and feelings and to develop their response to music through dance, by using rhythmic responses and contrasts of speed, shape, direction and level.

(DfES, 1995)

BOX 3.5 NATIONAL CURRICULUM FOR PHYSICAL EDUCATION 1995 – KEY STAGE 2 (DFES, 1995)

General requirements for Key Stage 2

1.   To promote physical activity and healthy lifestyles:
     a.   to be physically active;
     b.   to adopt the best possible posture and the appropriate use of the body;

c. to engage in activities that develop cardiovascular health, flexibility, muscular strength and endurance.

2. To develop positive attitudes, pupils should be taught:

a. to observe the conventions of fair play, honest competition and good sporting behaviour as individual participants, team members and spectators;
b. how to cope with success and limitations in performance;
c. to try hard to consolidate their performance;
d. to be mindful of others and the environment.

3. To ensure safe practice, pupils should be taught:

a. to respond readily to instructions;
b. to recognise and follow relevant rules, laws, codes and etiquette and safety procedures for different activities or events, in practice and during competition;
c. about the safety risks of wearing inappropriate clothing, footwear and jewellery and why particular clothing, footwear and protection are worn for different activities;
d. how to lift, carry, place and use equipment safely;
e. to warm up for and recover from exercise.

Key Stage 2

Areas of activity

Pupils should be taught:

Games

a. To understand and play small-sided games and simplified versions of recognised competitive team and individual games. Covering the following types – invasion, e.g. mini soccer, netball, striking and fielding e.g. rounders, small-sided cricket, net/wall, e.g. short tennis.
b. Common skills and principles, including attack and defence, in invasion, striking/fielding, net/wall and target games.
c. To improve the skills of sending, receiving, striking and travelling with a ball in the above games.

Gymnastic activities

a. Different means of turning, rolling, swinging, jumping, climbing, balancing and weight on hands and feet, and how to adapt, practice and refine these actions, both on the floor and using apparatus.

b. To emphasise changes of shape, speed and direction through gymnastic actions.

c. To practise refine and repeat a longer sequence of actions making increasingly complex movement sequences, both on the floor and using apparatus.

Dance

a. To compose and control their movements by varying shape, size, direction, level, speed, tension and continuity.

b. A number of dance forms from different times and places, including some traditional dances of the British Isles.

c. To express feelings, moods and ideas, to respond to music, and to create simple characters and narratives in response to a range of stimuli, through dance.

Athletic activities

a. To develop and refine basic techniques in running, e.g. over short distances, over longer distances, in relays, e.g. for accuracy and distance, and jumping, e.g. for height/distance, using a variety of equipment.

b. To measure, compare and improve their own performance.

Outdoor and adventurous activities

a. To perform outdoor and adventurous activities, e.g. orienteering exercises, in one or more different environments, e.g. playground, school grounds, parks, woodland, seashore.

b. Challenges of physical and problem solving nature, e.g. negotiating obstacle courses, using suitable equipment, e.g. gymnastic or adventure play apparatus, whilst working individually and with others.

c. The skills necessary for the activities undertaken.

Swimming

a. To swim unaided, competently and safely, for at least 25 metres.

b. To develop confidence in water, and how to rest , float and adopt support positions.

c. A variety of means of propulsion using either arms or legs or both, and how to develop effective and efficient swimming strokes on the front and the back.

d. The principles and skills of water safety and survival.

(DfES, 1995)

BOX 3.6 NATIONAL CURRICULUM FOR PHYSICAL EDUCATION 1995 – ATTAINMENT TARGETS (DFES, 1995)

End of Key Stage descriptions

Key Stage 1

Pupils plan and perform simple skills safely and show control in linking actions together. They improve their performance through practising their skills, working alone and with a partner. They talk about what they and others have done, and are able to make simple judgements. They recognise and describe the changes that happen in their bodies during exercise.

Key Stage 2

Pupils find solutions, sometimes responding imaginatively to the various challenges that they encounter in the different areas of activity. They practise, improve and refine performance, and repeat series of movements they have performed previously, with increasing control and accuracy. They work safely alone, in pairs and in groups, and as a member of a team. They make simple judgements about their own and other's performance, and use this information effectively to improve the accuracy, quality and variety of their own performance. They sustain energetic activity over appropriate periods of time, and demonstrate that they understand what is happening to their bodies during exercise.

(DfES, 1995)

However more important than the process here was the timing of the drafting of the new orders. During this period, the Conservative government of the mid-1990s, headed by Prime Minister John Major, sought to relaunch itself, under the maxim of 'Back to Basics'. Educational policy became dominated by the New Right which had a traditional, restorationist agenda (Ball, 1994; Kelly, 1999) echoing the Black Papers of a quarter of a century earlier. Critically for Physical Education, this period saw the publication of *Sport: Raising the Game* (DNH, 1995) which extolled the virtues of participating in competitive team games and sport, the ideals of which were firmly rooted in the Victorian era (see Mangan, 1981), As a consequence the 1995 revision of the National Curriculum 'was a narrow curriculum experience' (Green, 2008: 36) in which games was afforded a superior status in both time and importance and other activity areas became subordinate (Penney and Evans, 1999; 2005).

Under the Labour Government that followed, a further revision of the primary curriculum occurred in 1999 which restored a degree of balance and within Physical Education rescinded the superiority held by games over other activity areas. Furthermore, there was a strengthening of the process to be engaged upon within each area, specified as Acquiring and Developing

Skills, Selecting and Applying Skills, Evaluating and Improving Performance, Knowledge and Understanding of Fitness and Health (DfEE/QCA, 1999). (See Boxes 3.7 to 3.9 for more details.)

Despite the lack of overt references to sport and competitive team games in the 1999 national curriculum for Physical Education, subsequent policy statements have sought to reinforce a pro-sport ideology (Houlihan, 2002). This is most clearly seen in both the implementation of the Physical Education, School Sport and Club Links (PESSCL) strategy and the later Physical Education and Sport Strategy for Young People (PESSYP). In October 2002 the launch of the PESSCL strategy pledged to invest in excess of £1½ billion into Physical Education and School Sport within the UK. The strategy contained eight different strands (Specialist Sports Colleges, Sport Co-ordinators, Gifted

---

BOX 3.7 NATIONAL CURRICULUM FOR PHYSICAL EDUCATION 1999 – KEY STAGE 1 (DFEE/QCA, 1999)

Knowledge, skills and understanding

Acquiring and developing skills

1. Pupils should be taught to:
    a. explore basic skills, actions and ideas with increasing understanding;
    b. remember and repeat simple skills and actions with increasing control and coordination.

Selecting and applying skills, tactics and compositional ideas

2. Pupils should be taught to:
    a. explore how to choose and apply skills and actions in sequence and in combination;
    b. vary the way they perform skills by using simple tactics and movement phrases;
    c. apply rules and conventions for different activities.

Evaluating and improving performance

3. Pupils should be taught to:
    a. describe what they have done;
    b. observe, describe and copy what others have done;
    c. use what they have learnt to improve the quality and control of their work.

Knowledge and understanding of fitness and health

4. Pupils should be taught:
    a. how important it is to be active;
    b. to recognise and describe how their bodies feel during different activities.

Breadth of study

5. During the key stage, pupils should be taught the knowledge, skills and understanding through dance activities, games activities and gymnastic activities.

Dance activities

6. Pupils should be taught to:
    a. use movement imaginatively, responding to stimuli, including music, and performing basic skills [for example, travelling, being still, making a shape, jumping, turning and gesturing];
    b. change the rhythm, speed, level and direction of their movements;
    c. create and perform dances using simple movement patterns, including those from different times and cultures;
    d. express and communicate ideas and feelings.

Games activities

7. Pupils should be taught to:
    a. travel with, send and receive a ball and other equipment in different ways;
    b. develop these skills for simple net, striking/fielding and invasion-type games;
    c. play simple, competitive net, striking/fielding and invasion-type games that they and others have made, using simple tactics for attacking and defending.

Gymnastic activities

8. Pupils should be taught to:
    a. perform basic skills in travelling, being still, finding space and using it safely, both on the floor and using apparatus;
    b. develop the range of their skills and actions [for example, balancing, taking off and landing, turning and rolling];
    c. choose and link skills and actions in short movement phrases;

d.   create and perform short, linked sequences that show a clear beginning, middle and end and have contrasts in direction, level and speed.

Swimming activities and water safety

9.   Pupils should be taught to:
a.   move in water [for example, jump, walk, hop and spin, using swimming aids and support];
b.   float and move with and without swimming aids;
c.   feel the buoyancy and support of water and swimming aids;
d.   propel themselves in water using different swimming aids, arm and leg actions and basic strokes.

(DfEE/QCA, 1999)

BOX 3.8 NATIONAL CURRICULUM FOR PHYSICAL EDUCATION 1999 – KEY STAGE 2 (DFEE/QCA, 1999)

Knowledge, skills and understanding

Acquiring and developing skills

1.   Pupils should be taught to:
a.   consolidate their existing skills and gain new ones;
b.   perform actions and skills with more consistent control and quality.

Selecting and applying skills, tactics and compositional ideas

2.   Pupils should be taught to:
a.   plan, use and adapt strategies, tactics and compositional ideas for individual, pair, small-group and small-team activities;
b.   develop and use their knowledge of the principles behind the strategies, tactics and ideas to improve their effectiveness;
c.   apply rules and conventions for different activities.

Evaluating and improving performance

3.   Pupils should be taught to:
a.   identify what makes a performance effective;
b.   suggest improvements based on this information.

Knowledge and understanding of fitness and health

4. Pupils should be taught:
    a. how exercise affects the body in the short term;
    b. to warm up and prepare appropriately for different activities;
    c. why physical activity is good for their health and well-being;
    d. why wearing appropriate clothing and being hygienic is good for their health and safety.

Breadth of study

5. During the key stage, pupils should be taught the knowledge, skills and understanding through five areas of activity:
    a. dance activities;
    b. games activities;
    c. gymnastic activities;
    and two activity areas from:
    d. swimming activities and water safety;
    e. athletic activities;
    f. outdoor and adventurous activities.

Swimming activities and water safety must be chosen as one of these areas of activity unless pupils have completed the full Key Stage 2 teaching requirements in relation to swimming activities and water safety during Key Stage 1.

Dance activities

6. Pupils should be taught to:
    a. create and perform dances using a range of movement patterns, including those from different times, places and cultures;
    b. respond to a range of stimuli and accompaniment.

Games activities

7. Pupils should be taught to:
    a. play and make up small-sided and modified competitive net, striking/fielding and invasion games;
    b. use skills and tactics and apply basic principles suitable for attacking and defending;
    c. work with others to organise and keep the games going.

Gymnastic activities

8. Pupils should be taught to:
    a. create and perform fluent sequences on the floor and using apparatus;
    b. include variations in level, speed and direction in their sequences.

Swimming activities and water safety

9. Pupils should be taught to:
    a. pace themselves in floating and swimming challenges related to speed, distance and personal survival;
    b. swim unaided for a sustained period of time over a distance of at least 25 metres;
    c. use recognised arm and leg actions, lying on their front and back;
    d. use a range of recognised strokes and personal survival skills [for example, front crawl, back crawl, breaststroke, sculling, floating and surface diving].

Athletic activities

10. Pupils should be taught to:
    a. take part in and design challenges and competitions that call for precision, speed, power or stamina;
    b. use running, jumping and throwing skills both singly and in combination;
    c. pace themselves in these challenges and competitions.

Outdoor and adventurous activities

11. Pupils should be taught to:
    a. take part in outdoor activity challenges, including following trails, in familiar, unfamiliar and changing environments;
    b. use a range of orienteering and problem-solving skills;
    c. work with others to meet the challenges.

(DfEE/QCA, 1999)

BOX 3.9 ATTAINMENT TARGETS FOR THE NATIONAL CURRICULUM FOR PHYSICAL EDUCATION 1999 – LEVELS 1–4 (DFEE/QCA, 1999)

Level 1

Pupils copy, repeat and explore simple skills and actions with basic control and coordination. They start to link these skills and actions in ways that suit the activities. They describe and comment on their own and others' actions. They talk about how to exercise safely, and how their bodies feel during an activity.

Level 2

Pupils explore simple skills. They copy, remember, repeat and explore simple actions with control and coordination. They vary skills, actions and ideas and link these in ways that suit the activities. They begin to show some understanding of simple tactics and basic compositional ideas. They talk about differences between their own and others' performance and suggest improvements. They understand how to exercise safely, and describe how their bodies feel during different activities.

Level 3

Pupils select and use skills, actions and ideas appropriately, applying them with coordination and control. They show that they understand tactics and composition by starting to vary how they respond. They can see how their work is similar to and different from others' work, and use this understanding to improve their own performance. They give reasons why warming up before an activity is important, and why physical activity is good for their health.

Level 4

Pupils link skills, techniques and ideas and apply them accurately and appropriately. Their performance shows precision, control and fluency, and that they understand tactics and composition. They compare and comment on skills, techniques and ideas used in their own and others' work, and use this understanding to improve their performance. They explain and apply basic safety principles in preparing for exercise. They describe what effects exercise has on their bodies, and how it is valuable to their fitness and health.

(DfEE/QCA, 1999)

and Talented, Investigating PE and School Sport, Step into Sport, Professional Development, School/Club Links and Swimming). With its overall objective to enhance the take-up of sporting opportunities by 5–16 year-olds a public service agreement (PSA) pledged to engage children in at least two hours high quality PE and sport at school each week (DfES/DCMS, 2003). The expectation on staff to increase their delivery time was raised still further with the injection of another £¾ billion through the introduction of PESSYP which pledged to create a new '5 hour offer' for all (DCSF, 2008).

At the same time as these policy initiatives were developed the curriculum in England underwent significant change but strangely not as a joined up or as a co-ordinated strategy but as isolated pieces of engineering at either end of the educational continuum. At the very earliest stage, May 2008 saw the introduction of the Early Years Foundation Stage (EYFS) framework, which provided the statutory requirements for setting the standards for learning, development and care for children from 0–5 years. The framework aimed at laying a secure foundation for future learning through learning and development and was planned around six areas: Personal, Social and Emotional Development; Communication, Language and Literacy; Problem Solving, Reasoning and Numeracy; Knowledge and Understanding of the World; Physical Development; and Creative Development (QCDA, 2008). This was retained and revised by the Coalition government in 2012 (DfE, 2012).

At the other end of the age range, a new secondary curriculum for England was published in 2007 and came into effect in September 2008, as part of a wider review of 14–19 education. As previously, a single subject approach was advocated with the biggest change evident in the change of language. Gone went activity areas and strands and in came a 'Range of Content' identified as outwitting opponents, accurate replication, exploring and communicating ideas concepts and emotions, performing at maximum levels, identifying and solving problems and exercising safely and effectively. Through this range of content, 'Key Concepts' (competency, performance, creativity and healthy active lifestyles) and 'Key Processes' (developing skills in physical activity, making and applying decisions, developing physical and mental capacity, evaluating and improving and making informed choices about healthy active lifestyles) were to be fostered (QCA, 2007). Importantly, what was created shared little or no similarity in structure between the primary National Curriculum or the newly devised EYFS framework highlighting some significant disconnections.

A disconnected curriculum: a cause for concern

A consequence of focusing on a pro-sport ideology and more elite performance in practical terms is that policies such as the PESSCL and PESSYP strategy emerge as clear 'top-down' models with a large majority of the time, money and resources being directed into the secondary sector. The 'top-down' model was again apparent within the revised secondary curriculum and begged the question of how continuity and progression can realistically be achieved and how such a radical shift can result in greater 'connectivity' sought at the launch of National Association for Physical Education only two years earlier (Talbot, 2006: 30).

Perhaps the most serious concern of any disconnected curriculum is the reaching of the 'proficiency barrier' through which children find it difficult to move, caused by the absence of progressive steps that permit children to move from the simple activities of the early years to the more complex activities of later childhood and beyond (NASPE, 1995; Jess et al., 2004). In short, if children are unable to efficiently perform basic physical competencies such as throwing and catching a ball, they will find it difficult to participate successfully in physical activities that require these skills at a later time. Ecological approaches to studying motor development of children have revealed that mature movement patterns are influenced not only by maturation but also by environmental factors including equipment, cue information and feedback (Goodway et al., 2002; Langerdorfer and Robertson, 2002; Southard, 2002; Whitall, 2003), 'thus refuting the "it happens naturally" misconception' (Bailey et al., 2009: 8). With the most significant periods of development taking place almost entirely within the primary age range (Gallahue and Ozmun, 1995) putting the right building blocks in place from the bottom up, builds a much stronger and sustainable curriculum model (see Gallahue and Ozmun, 1995; Almond, 1997; Jess et al., 2004; Haydn-Davies, 2005; Griggs, 2007).

Gaining progressive experiences of competency are clearly important conditions for lifetime participation in movement culture. According to Crum (1993: 342) 'for such a satisfying and lasting participation, one must develop a repertoire of skills and knowledge so that exercising, playing, dancing, or sporting is possible without disgracing oneself and/or disturbing other participants. This competency repertoire does not come naturally to individuals; it can only be acquired in structured learning processes.' It is suggested by Crum (1993) that five key strands of learning should be used to maximise the reconnection between different policy agendas and avoid future disconnections by allowing for a coherent yet flexible plan across the age ranges. Affective development, technomotor, sociomotor, cognitive and reflective competencies should form the key framework upon which to hang the chronological design of learning activities, providing a coherent platform from which practitioners can create progression and continuity. Their connection with wider movement culture should enable schools to deliver a broad range of activities, the rationale of the selection of which must centre upon pupils' needs and school facilities.

In search of perspectives on how to approach a new vision for primary Physical Education, one might venture to look across the border. Since devolution, Wales has opted to produce its own curriculum (all previous iterations were written for England and Wales), the most recent of which was published in 2008. In many ways it remains similar to the current orders in England, being largely focused on skills and competencies and is discreetly taught in separate subjects.

However, interestingly there is a repositioning of the content, which is grouped into such themes as creative, health fitness and well being and a shows greater commitment to cross-curricular links (DCELLS, 2008).

By contrast, to date, the curriculum is non-statutory in Scotland and so is not dictated by the Government. Responsibility for what is taught rests with local authorities and schools, taking into account national guidelines and advice. However, more recently through its strategy of Curriculum for Excellence a concerted effort has been made to provide a more coherent, flexible and enriched curriculum from 3 to 18. Launched in 2010/11, the curriculum is laid out in eight major areas: Expressive Arts, Health and Well Being, Languages, Mathematics, Religious and Moral Education, Sciences, Social Studies and Technologies. Of relevance here 'Physical Education, Physical Activity and Sport' can be located in the area of Health and Well Being (see also Chapter 8), along with five other topics: Mental, Emotional, Social and Physical Well Being, Planning for Choices and Changes, Food and Health, Substance Misuse, and Relationships, Sexual Health and Parenthood (LTS, 2009). What has been of interest in both Wales and Scotland has been the shift back towards a more holistic viewpoint and a child-centred approach, echoing HMI recommendations of the mid-1980s. This was set to happen in England until the political landscape suddenly changed.

After almost a decade, the Labour government commissioned Sir Jim Rose, former director of inspection at Ofsted, to head up a review of the primary curriculum in England. In April 2009, what has commonly been referred to as the 'Rose Review' was published (DCSF, 2009). Here Physical Education was located under a holistic looking umbrella of 'Understanding Physical Development, Health and Well Being'. Furthermore, specific activities such as Dance were given greater focus under another heading of 'Understanding the Arts'. Clear synergies were also apparent between the Rose Review and the underpinning EYFS strategy. However with the coming to power of the coalition government in 2010 all such plans were scrapped. In the void that was the left, the primary national curriculum for Physical Education remained vulnerable. Unchanged for over a decade with a new government and a Secretary of State keen to make a mark, the next big idea would undoubtedly make an impact. The catalyst for change came in the form of the London Olympic Games held in the summer of 2012.

Curriculum 2014: 'policy by the way'

Since the revival of the modern Olympic Games in 1896, resulting legacies have occurred in range of forms most commonly by the way of physical structure or artefact (Cashman, 1998). Yet it can sometimes be the social impact and the resulting behaviours than can be as equally as durable and arguably more powerful (Ritchie, 2000). In recent decades the practice of setting out legacy commitments by host cities and their respective governments has become standard practice, illustrated ahead of the Summer Olympic and Paralympic

Games that was held in London in 2012 (DCMS, 2007). A central tenet within the London legacy commitments was how the Games was to 'Inspire a generation of young people' (DCMS, 2007). Both during the Games and in its aftermath government rhetoric was awash in the media concerning the different ways in which our young people were going to be inspired. Significantly however it was on 11 August 2012, on the eve of the close of the Games, that the UK Prime Minister, David Cameron, published a statement on the Number 10 webpage stating that we will put 'competitive sport for children at the heart of Olympics legacy' (HM Government, 2012). Specifically it stated that any new national Physical Education curriculum which would follow the Games will now 'require every primary school child to take part in competitive team sport like football, netball and hockey'. This, despite the fact Britain has rarely entered the Olympic football competition, that netball is not an Olympic sport and that team games remain a minor part of any summer games' programme.

The impact and influence of a particular event or policy upon the planning of another is what Dery (1998: 163) has termed 'policy by the way.' Here dominant discourses and rhetoric are favoured and permitted often without understanding the appropriateness or impact that may result. Where these impacts are most sharply felt are in crowded and contested policy spaces.

As Physical Education finds itself, as a curriculum subject, in an arguably unique position, in a 'crowded and contested policy space' (Penney, 2008: 35) with felt pressures from three competing discourses and policy areas, namely sport, education and health (Houlihan and Green, 2006) (as discussed in Chapter 2), it is susceptible to being pulled in a particular direction. The realisation of the impact of the Olympic legacy became apparent when on 7 February 2013 the Rt Hon Michael Gove MP, Secretary of State for Education, launched a public consultation on the government's proposals for the reform of the national curriculum in England. This followed a review of the national curriculum which was launched in January 2011 with the aims of ensuring that the new national curriculum embodies rigour and high standards and creates coherence in what is taught in schools; ensuring that all children are taught the essential knowledge in the key subject disciplines and beyond that core, to allow teachers greater freedom to use their professionalism and expertise to help all children realise their potential (DfE, 2013a). From this consultation emerged the framework document for the national curriculum in England (DfE, 2013b) outlining the Programmes of Study (PoS) for each subject to be implemented from September 2014. (The PoS for Key Stages 1 and 2 is shown in Box 3.10.)

The implications of this change of course will take time to emerge but given well-established behaviours over the last decade some predictions it could be argued are fairly safe. First, schools that were already delivering a broad and varied curriculum under the 1999 iteration of the NCPE encompassing dance, gymnastics, dance, games, Outdoor and Adventurous Activities (OAA) and swimming are likely to continue to do so because the new curriculum allows them the freedom to do so. Similarly if they believed that good practice was in

BOX 3.10 NATIONAL CURRICULUM FOR PHYSICAL EDUCATION 2014 – KEY STAGE 1 AND 2 (DFE, 2013B)

Purpose of study

A high-quality physical education curriculum inspires all pupils to succeed and excel in competitive sport and other physically demanding activities. It should provide opportunities for pupils to become physically confident in a way which supports their health and fitness. Opportunities to compete in sport and other activities build character and help to embed values such as fairness and respect.

Aims

The national curriculum for physical education aims to ensure that all pupils:
* develop competence to excel in a broad range of physical activities;
* are physically active for sustained periods of time;
* engage in competitive sports and activities;
* lead healthy, active lives.

Attainment targets

By the end of each key stage, pupils are expected to know, apply and understand the matters, skills and processes specified in the relevant programme of study. Schools are not required by law to teach the example content in [square brackets].

Subject content

Key Stage 1

Pupils should develop fundamental movement skills, become increasingly competent and confident and access a broad range of opportunities to extend their agility, balance and coordination, individually and with others. They should be able to engage in competitive (both against self and against others) and co-operative physical activities, in a range of increasingly challenging situations.
Pupils should be taught to:
* master basic movements including running, jumping, throwing and catching, as well as developing balance, agility and co-ordination, and begin to apply these in a range of activities;
* participate in team games, developing simple tactics for attacking and defending;
* perform dances using simple movement patterns.

Key Stage 2

Pupils should continue to apply and develop a broader range of skills, learning how to use them in different ways and to link them to make actions and sequences of movement. They should enjoy communicating, collaborating and competing with each other. They should develop an understanding of how to improve in different physical activities and sports and learn how to evaluate and recognise their own success.

Pupils should be taught to:
- use running, jumping, throwing and catching in isolation and in combination;
- play competitive games, modified where appropriate [for example, badminton, basketball, cricket, football, hockey, netball, rounders and tennis], and apply basic principles suitable for attacking and defending;
- develop flexibility, strength, technique, control and balance [for example, through athletics and gymnastics];
- perform dances using a range of movement patterns;
- take part in outdoor and adventurous activity challenges both individually and within a team;
- compare their performances with previous ones and demonstrate improvement to achieve their personal best.

(DfE, 2013b)

place when using the four strands (Acquiring and Developing Skills, Selecting and Applying Skills, Tactics and Compositional Ideas, Evaluating and Improving Performance' and Knowledge and Understanding of Fitness and Health) as a focus for lessons exemplified in the 1999 iteration of the NCPE, again this is likely to continue. By contrast, if schools continue to look for opportunities to reduce their delivery time and content then the lack of specification in the PoS will only further permit this to happen.

The increased focus on competition and in particular competitive teams now permeates down into Key Stage 1 and though this was seen in the narrowing of the 1995 iteration of the NCPE the implications for this focus given the current climate are considerable. One could speculate that building or attempting to build an elite system of Olympians upon the footings of primary Physical Education lessons opens the door still wider to external providers who are willing to become part of this popular post Olympic legacy. Subcontracting Physical Education lessons to 'the nearest confident person in a tracksuit' (Griggs, 2010: 45) who purports to be a specialist becomes legitimised by the language of increasing competition in traditional specialist sports. Should further money be made available to National Governing Bodies (NGB) this shift will be further exacerbated.

Furthermore previous approaches which have directed Physical Education to concentrate on a narrow menu of competitive sports, have not been effective in maintaining young people's involvement in playing sport after leaving school (Green, 2002). The championing of traditional and recognisable British games by the Number 10 statement; football, netball and hockey, within a desire for establishing an Olympic legacy, ignores our proven track record of medal winning sports: rowing, cycling, sailing, athletics and equestrian events. If the objective is to promote competitiveness in Olympic team games, a widening of the diet of specialist games to include, for example, basketball, handball and volleyball (prominent Olympic team games) would seem more logical (Griggs and Ward, 2013). Rather than narrowing Physical Education curricula there is a growing body of literature which calls for pupil experiences in school to reflect the dynamic culture of active-leisure preferences of young people (Green, 2012). Shoehorning Physical Education into a 'one size that fits all' approach of competitive sport and sustained physical activity assumes that the outcomes of competition and mechanised approaches to health are good and appropriate for all. Empirical evidence suggests otherwise (Evans, 2014).

THOUGHT BOX

If the main aim of primary Physical Education was to maximise the participation within physical activity through adolescence and then into adult life, then what should primary Physical Education look like? How realistic is it that primary Physical Education could deliver on this aim or on other suggested aims such as achieving more Olympic medals?

Conclusion

The desire of the current government that Physical Education must return to curricula focussed on competition within specialised traditional sports, couched in Olympic legacy rhetoric, hails a return to the contested terrain of the Black Papers. Physical Education curricula have historically fluctuated between an emphasis upon breadth and balance and a prescribed diet of narrow sporting activities. Policy has also demanded a focus upon competitive sport as a means to develop future sporting champions, in addition to alleviating contemporary concerns with increasing sedentary behaviour by training pupils to adopt lifelong participation in physical activity. Sadly, rather than the 2014 NCPE being based upon substantive evidence to develop primary Physical Education, government statements and resulting policies appear to be 'policy by the way' attached to the rhetoric of public health concerns and Olympic legacy.

KEY READINGS

This chapter illustrates that the creation of any iteration of the National Curriculum for Physical Education is wrapped up in complex political and socio-cultural issues. Arguably the best account shedding insight into this world was provided by Evans, J. and Penney, D. (1995) The politics of pedagogy: making a National Curriculum Physical Education 1, *Journal of Education Policy*, 10(1), 27–44. Further explanation as to how the legacy of London 2012 Olympic Games has shaped recent primary Physical Education policy can be found in Griggs, G. and Ward, G. (2013) The London 2012 legacy for primary Physical Education: policy by the way?, *Sociological Research Online*, 18(3), 13. Those looking for the most recent Physical Education curriculum documents in England should go to www.gov.uk/government/publications/national-curriculum-in-england-physical-education-programmes-of-study. Historical copies, including the 1999 iteration, are now available from the National Archives. Each subject, including Physical Education can be accessed at http://webarchive.nationalarchives.gov.uk/20100202100434/http:/curriculum.qcda.gov.uk/key-stages-1-and-2/subjects/index.aspx.

References

Almond, L. (1997) *Physical Education in Schools* (2nd edition). London: Kogan Page.

Bailey, R., Armour, K., Kirk, D., Jess, M., Pickup, I., Sandford, R. and BERA Physical Education and Sport Pedagogy Special Interest Group (2009). The educational benefits claimed for physical education and school sport: an academic review, *Research Papers in Education*, 24(1), 1–27.

Ball, S.J. (1994) *Education Reform: A Critical and Post-structural Approach*. Buckingham: Open University Press.

Campbell, R. and Neill, S. (1992) *Teacher Time and Curriculum Manageability at Key Stage 1. Third Report on Research into the Use of Teacher Time*. London: AMMA.

Cashman, R. (1998) Olympic legacy in an Olympic City: monuments, museums and memory. Proceedings of the fourth international symposium for Olympic research. Canada: The University of Western Ontario.

Central Advisory Council for Education (CACE) (1967) *Children and Their Primary Schools (The Plowden Report)*. London: HMSO.

Cox, C.B. and Dyson, A.E. (eds) (1969a) *Fight for Education: Black Paper 1*. London: Critical Quarterly Society.

Cox, C.B. and Dyson, A.E. (eds) (1969b) *Crisis in Education: Black Paper 2*. London: Critical Quarterly Society.

Crum, B. (1993) Conventional thought and practice in Physical Education: problems of teaching and implications for change, *Quest*, 45, 339–356.

Department for Children, Education, Lifelong Learning and Skills (DCELLS) (2008) *Physical Education in the National Curriculum for Wales*. Cardiff: DCELLS.

Department for Children, Schools and Families (DCSF) (2008) *Physical Education and Sport Strategy for Young People*. London: DCSF.

Department for Children, Schools and Families (DCSF) (2009) *Independent Review of the Primary Curriculum: Final Report (The Rose Review)*. London: DCSF.

Department for Culture Media and Sport (DCMS) (2007) *Our promise for 2012. How will the UK benefit from the Olympic Games and Paralympic Games*. London: DCMS.

Department for Education (DfE) (2012) *Statutory Framework for the Early Years Foundation Stage*. London: DfE.

Department for Education (DfE) (2013a) *National curriculum review: new programmes of study and attainment targets from September 2014*. London: DfE.

Department for Education (DfE) (2013b) *The national curriculum in England: Framework document*. London: DfE.

Department for Education and Employment/Qualifications and Curriculum Authority (DfEE/QCA) (1999) *The National Curriculum in England: Physical Education*. London: HMSO.

Department of Education and Science (DES) (1985) *The Curriculum From 5–16. Curriculum Matters 2*. London: HMSO.

Department of Education and Science (DES) (1991) *Physical Education for Age 5–16*. London: DES.

Department for Education and Skills (DfES) (1995) *National Curriculum for Physical Education 1995*. London: DfES

Department for Education and Skills/Department for Culture, Media and Sport (DfES/DCMS) (2003) *Learning Through Physical Education and Sport: A Guide to the Physical Education, School Sport and Club Links Strategy*. London: DfES/DCMS.

Department of National Heritage (DNH) (1995) *Sport: Raising the Game*. London: DNH.

Dery, D. (1998). Policy by the way: when policy is incidental to making other policies, *Journal of Public Policy*, 18, 163–176.

Educational Reform Act (ERA) (1988) *Education Reform Act, 29 July 1988*. London: HMSO.

Evans, J. (2014). Equity and inclusion in physical education PLC, *European Physical Education Review*, doi: 10.1177/1356336X14524854.

Gallahue, D. and Ozmun, J. (1995) *Understanding Motor Development: Infants, Children, Adolescents, Adults* (3rd edition). Madison, WI: Brown and Benchmark.

Goodway, J.D., Rudisill, M.E. and Valentin, N.C. (2002). The influence of instruction on the development of catching in young children. In J.E. Clark and J. Humphrey (eds) *Motor Development: Research and Reviews: 2*, 96–119, Reston, VA: AAHPERD.

Green, K. (2002) Lifelong participation, physical education and the work of Ken Roberts, *Sport, Education and Society*, 7(2), 167–182.

Green, K. (2008) *Understanding Physical Education*. London: Sage.

Green, K. (2012) Mission impossible? Reflecting upon the relationship between physical education, youth sport and lifelong participation, *Sport, Education and Society*, 19(4), 357–375.

Griggs, G. (2007) Physical Education: primary matters, secondary importance. *Education 3–13*, 35(1), 59–69.

Griggs, G. (2010) For sale – primary Physical Education. £20 per hour or nearest offer, *Education 3–13*, 38(1), 39–46.

Griggs, G. and Ward, G. (2013) The London 2012 Legacy for primary Physical Education: policy by the way? *Sociological Research Online*, 18(3), 13.

Harnett, P. and Vinney, M. (2008) What has happened to curriculum breadth and balance in primary school. In P. Harnett (ed.) *Understanding Primary Education*. London: Routledge.

Haydn-Davies, D. (2005) How does the concept of physical literacy relate to what is and what could be the practice of Physical Education, *British Journal of Teaching Physical Education*, 36(3), 45–48.

HM Government (2012) Competitive sport for children at the heart of Olympics Legacy www.number10.gov.uk/news/competitive-sport-for-children-at-the-heart-of-olympics-legacy/ (accessed 4 March 2013).

Houlihan, B. (2002) Political involvement in sport, physical education and recreation. In A. Laker (ed.) *The Sociology of Sport and Physical Education: An Introductory Reader*. London: Routledge Falmer.

Houlihan, B. and Green, M. (2006) The changing status of school sport and physical education: explaining policy change, *Sport, Education and Society*, 11(1), 73–92.

Jess, M., Dewar, K. and Fraser, G. (2004) Basic moves: developing a foundation for lifelong physical activity, *British Journal of Teaching Physical Education*, 35(2), 23–27.

Kelly, A.V. (1999) *The Curriculum: Theory and Practice* (4th edition). London: Paul Chapman Publishing.

Langerdorfer. S.J. and Robertson, M.A. (2002) Developmental profiles in overarm throwing: searching for 'attractors', 'stages' and 'constraints'. In J.E. Clark and J. Humphrey (eds) *Motor Development: Research and Reviews: 2*, 1–25, Reston. VA: AAHPERD.

Learning and Teaching Scotland (LTS) (2009) *Curriculum for Excellence*. Edinburgh: LTS.

Mangan, J.A. (1981) *Athleticism in the Victorian and Edwardian Public School*. Cambridge: Cambridge University Press.

National Association for Physical Education (NASPE) (1995) *Moving Into the Future: National Physical Education Standards: A Guide to Content and Assessment*. St Louis, MI: Mosby.

Ofsted (1993) *History Key Stages 1, 2 and 3. Second Year 1992–1993*. London: HMSO

Oliver, A. (2004) Primary Education in England. In A. Browne and D. Haylock (eds) *Professional Issues for Primary Teachers*. London: Paul Chapman Publishing.

Penney, D. (2008) Playing a political game and play for position: policy and curriculum development in health and PE, *European PE Review*, 4(1), 33–49.

Penney, D. and Evans, J. (1999) *Politics, Policy and Practice in Physical Education*. London: E & FN Spon.

Penney, D. and Evans, J. (2005) Policy, power and politics in Physical Education. In K. Green and K. Hardman (eds) *Physical Education: Essential Issues*. London: Sage.

QCA (2007) *The National Curriculum for Physical Education at Key Stage 3 and 4* (online). Available online at http://curriculum.qcda.gov.uk/ (accessed 10 November 2009).

QCDA (2008) *Early Years Foundation Stage Framework*. London: QCDA.

Rawling, E. (2001) The politics and practicalities of Curriculum change 1991–2000: issues arising from a study of school Geography in England, *British Journal of Educational Studies*, 49(2), 137–158.

Ritchie, J.R.B. (2000) Turning 16 days into 16 years through, Olympic legacies, *Event Management*, 6(3), 155–166.

School Curriculum and Assessment Authority (SCAA) (1994) *The Review of the National Curriculum. A Report on the 1994 Consultation*. London: SCAA.

Southard, D. (2002) Control parameters for the development of throwing. In J.E. Clark and J. Humphrey (eds) *Motor Development: Research and Review* (2nd edition). Reston, VA: AAHPERD.

Talbot, M. (2006) afPE news: progress and challenges for the Association, *Physical Education Matters*, 1(1), 30.

Webb, R. (1993) *Eating the Elephant Bit by Bit: The National Curriculum at Key Stage 2. Final Report Commissioned by the Association of Teachers and Lecturers*. London: ATL Publishers.

Whitall, J. (2003) Development of locomotor co-ordination and control in children. In G. Ravelsbergh, K. Davids, J. van der Kamp and S. Bennett (eds) *Development of Movement Co-ordination in Children*. London: Routledge.

4

PRIMARY TEACHER TRAINING AND CONTINUING PROFESSIONAL DEVELOPMENT

Introduction

Globally concerns have been raised about both primary teacher training (commonly referred to as either Initial Teacher Training (ITT) or Initial Teacher Education (ITE)), and ongoing support for primary school teachers (commonly referred to as CPD (continuing professional development)) especially in their capability to deliver effective Physical Education (Hardman and Marshall, 2005; Green, 2008). Analysis of the history of teacher education in the UK reveals a picture of erratic and incoherent change, driven by both providers of training and, more significantly, overarching power of government policy from both sides of the political divide (Wetz, 2010). Arguably the most significant policy document produced in this area in the last 25 years has been The Department for Education Circular 9/92 (DfE, 1992), which represented a watershed in contemporary teacher education, itemising the first list of competencies which trainees were required to fulfil by spending less time in university and significantly increased time in schools, under the direct supervision of a serving teacher. Modern preoccupations of being able to account for different aspects of knowledge, teaching and assessment have seen revisions of these competencies and further published as the Professional Standards for Qualified Teacher Status (TDA, 2008). Concerns have been raised that this cultural shift has reduced teaching to the acquisition of craft skills and retreated to a set of reductionist and functional competencies (Alexander, 2008; Wetz, 2010) and, as a result, the role of the teacher has regressed to that of technician (Giroux, 2009). Yet successive governments have asserted that a 36-week course during a single year remains sufficient preparation to become a reflective, effective and visionary professional (Giroux, 2009; Wetz, 2010).

Issues within primary Physical Education teacher training

Research suggests that a number of issues have emerged from the shifting landscape within primary Physical Education teacher training and these will be briefly examined next, starting with the issue of time.

Time

In England there has been a steady reduction in the time spent on Physical Education in primary teacher training over the last 25 years with a wide variation of durations recorded, becoming as low as five hours in postgraduate programmes (Caldecott et al., 2006a, 2006b; Carney and Armstrong 1996; Clay, 1999; Ofsted, 2000; PEA, 1984; SCOPE, 1991; Warburton, 2001; Williams, 1985). The reaction to this reduction in time triggered proposals for statutory minimum durations given to Physical Education during primary teacher training, ranging from a minimum of 60 hours (BCPE, 1980; CCPR/NAHT, 1992; PEA UK 1987), to later proposals of 25 hours (Sport England, 2002) and 30 hours (CCPR, 2004).

Quality of training

It is acknowledged that the quality of teacher training is not just about the volume of contact time (Pickup, 2006), but 'also about the philosophical approach to and content of the training' (Harris et al., 2012: 369). Unevenness and imbalance in content, for example, have been a feature of curriculum design for some time (Ofsted, 1998; Capel and Katene, 2000) with a greater focus towards games activities, some attention given to gymnastics and dance and minimal attention (and in some cases none) given to OAA, athletics (Ofsted, 1998, 2005; Warburton, 2001) or swimming (*Times Educational Supplement/ Central Council for Physical Recreation*, 2003). Most worryingly perhaps are the health and safety concerns that result from a lack of training. Such concerns led Ofsted (2000) to recommend that trainees should have experience in the two 'most dangerous' elements – namely OAA and swimming – yet Caldecott et al. (2006b) found that on 60 per cent of PGCE courses, these areas were not covered. For Ofsted (2005: 3), the lack of adequate training becomes most apparent in the core knowledge of teachers and hinders further progress being made:

> Weak subject knowledge limits further improvement … many lack confidence in allowing pupils the freedom to explore and plan their own movements; this is particularly evident in potentially challenging situations … Weak subject knowledge also limits teachers' ability to intervene and correct pupils' quality of work, and to refine and modify tasks according to pupils' needs.

The low level of teacher confidence indicated by Ofsted has been a recurring feature of more recent research and looks set to continue (DeCorby et al., 2005; Griggs, 2010; Morgan and Bourke, 2005; 2008). Of concern is that the cycle of poor student preparation is continually reinforced by mentors who have suffered similar scarce preparation and who often are reluctant teachers of Physical Education (Morgan and Bourke, 2005, 2008; Pickup, 2006; Stroot and Ko, 2006).

Lack of teaching practice

Research papers and reports indicate that trainee primary school teachers teach very few Physical Education lessons during their training period (Caldecott et al., 2006a, 2006b; Haydn-Davies, 2008; Ofsted, 2000; Rolfe, 2001; Rolfe and Chedzoy, 1997). Indeed, Pickup (2006) described trainee teachers' school-based experiences as at best adequate and at worst non-existent. The most recent insight into this area was provided by Haydn-Davies and Spence (2010), who conducted an investigation into trainee teachers' opportunities to teach Physical Education during their training, carried out across three universities. The research confirmed that opportunities to practise teaching Physical Education and observe others teaching were not offered or possibly taken by a significant number of trainees. More than half the trainees did not teach more than one lesson of Physical Education during their training and, on average, a quarter of trainees did not teach any Physical Education while on placement. The study concluded that there was a lack of enthusiasm to teach Physical Education in too many primary schools, poor mentoring of trainees in relation to Physical Education, a lack of good teaching examples and too few opportunities to observe good practice.

Reliance on prior sporting experiences

Childhood and adolescent experiences within sport and physical education have been shown to have a compelling influence upon teachers' conceptions of the activities they deliver during physical education lessons (Capel, 2007). These experiences produce a set of robust beliefs about what they expect to experience during their training (be it positive or negative) and this can serve to reinforce rather than to challenge their existing viewpoint (Doolittle er al., 1993; Lawson, 1983a, 1983b; Solmon and Ashy, 1995). Beliefs formed by trainee Physical Education teachers prior to their training are not easily changed and research suggests that teacher training has relatively little impact on trainee teachers (Evans et al., 1996; Green, 1998; Curtner-Smith, 1999; Tsangaridou, 2006).

It is perhaps understandable that when faced with a crisis of confidence, teachers revert to their own personal experiences of being taught, and this has manifested itself in the over-reliance of teaching skills and techniques learned largely during their secondary education or from external sporting encounters or occasionally limited training experiences (Capel, 2007; Ofsted, 2004, 2005, 2009; Kirk, 2010; Ward, 2011). A direct consequence is the perpetuation of lessons in which children are being 'busy, happy, and good' (Placek, 1983) with very little or no consideration of theoretical underpinning (Tinning, 2006). Unfortunately there is little to break this cycle of practice when student teachers are provided with little time to reflect upon their own beliefs and practices (Rossi and Cassidy, 1999; Darling-Hammond, 2000; Hobson, 2002; Stroot and Ko, 2006) and student teachers are provided with scant opportunity for critical reflection of how trainees' experiences as learners influence their beliefs and approaches to teaching (Hardy, 1999; Burgess, 2000; Wetz, 2010).

These experiences, beliefs and values about the nature of Physical Education become crystallised through a process of occupational socialisation during initial training placements and first professional appointments and continue to grow in structure and size as trainee teacher's perceptions of their role are shaped by their colleagues and the structures within which they are required to work (Lawson, 1983a,1983b; Curtner-Smith et al., 2008). Within this process, coaching courses and personal experiences become dominant parts of their pedagogical content knowledge and this is reflected in their approaches to teaching (Stroot and Ko, 2006; Tsangaridou, 2006; Capel et al., 2009). Exploration and development of their pedagogical content knowledge is ignored in favour of the immediate need to assimilate to the practices of the schools in which they train and more significantly in the context in which they then work (Curtner-Smith et al., 2008). Consequently, most new entrants to teaching continue to teach what and how they were taught and any innovative ideas and practices developed during their training are pushed to one side and can become lost in the requirement to 'fit in' (Smyth, 1995; Curtner-Smith, 1997; Williams and Williamson, 1995, 1998; Capel, 2007.

THOUGHT BOX

Reflect on your own training in primary Physical Education. How well equipped were you? What else could have been provided in the time available?

Attempts at providing national continuing professional development for primary Physical Education

The most significant national CPD programme for primary Physical Education over the last 25 years has arguably been the TOPs programme. It was devised in a bid to help address the long-standing concerns in England about the adequacy of primary teacher training and classroom practice (Caldecott et al., 2006a, 2006b; Davies, 1999; Downey, 1979; Kerr and Rodgers, 1981; Morgan, 1997; Warburton, 2001; Wright, 2002). The TOPs programme was devised by the Youth Sport Trust (YST) and was introduced into primary schools in England from 1996, initially comprising two courses: TOP Play and TOP Sport (Youth Sport Trust, 1997). TOP Play focused on games activities for Key Stage 1 pupils and TOP Sport developed the TOP Play activities into a range of sports for Key Stage 2 pupils. Additional TOPs programmes such as TOP Dance, TOP Gymnastics and TOP OAA were later developed, as were revisions of the programme following the publication of the national curriculum for Physical Education (NCPE) in 1999 (DfEE/QCA, 1999). The overall programme had ambitious aims of raising the overall status and standards of Physical Education and school sport (Haskins, 2003). Teachers accessed the TOPs programmes by attending a four-hour course, which was largely practical in nature, during which they received a handbook, a set of cards and a bag of equipment to take back to their school. A further restructuring of the scheme occurred in 2005 when TOPs was integrated into the Professional Development Programme within the Physical Education, School Sport and Club Links (PESSCL) strategy (DCMS, 2003). It was then within the resulting School Sport Partnership (SSP) structure that alternative CPD provision began to be developed.

Significantly, the erosion of local government advisory services and the direction of funding though PESSCL and PESSYP development strands have further tied CPD to the delivery of specific policy. The injection of funding through these avenues has opened up a market economy of CPD, with a various national governing bodies (NGB) of sport, sports partnerships and commercial operators, entering the fray. By identifying perceived gaps in the market, a plethora of supporting resources has become available to teachers in either printed or human form via the employment of sports coaches (Griggs, 2008; Blair and Capel, 2008, 2011). In both cases the focus on sport-specific content, particularly the organisation of technical practices and provision of hints and tips, simply serves to provide legitimacy to Physical Education as sport techniques. It could be argued that the rise in the abundance of teacher-proof curriculum packages reaffirms the subordinate role of the teacher as delivery agent, relinquishing teaching to predetermined content and instructional procedure (Giroux, 2009).

Difficulties with CPD programmes

Research and reports into CPD programmes for primary Physical Education, including the TOPs programme, have continued to be less than positive (Spode, 1997; Graves, 2008; Hunt, 1998; Roberts et al., 1998; Lawrence, 2003; Ofsted, 2005; Harris et al., 2012). Furthermore, wide variations in provision have been reported across England, ranging from nothing to multiple days, fully resourced and spread over the school year (Woodhouse, 2006). The major flaw in CPD programmes is that they remain rooted in gaining information by attending an 'all you need to know' in a one-off, off-site, one-day course (Armour and Yelling, 2002). Such programmes are rooted in the whims of funding streams, unsystematic planning and often-present eclectic menus of contemporary fads and fashions (Armour and Yelling, 2004), resulting in 'fragmented and incoherent teacher learning that lacks intellectual rigour, fails to build on existing knowledge and skills, and does little to support teachers in the day-to-day challenges of improving student learning' (Sparks 2002: 91). Courses are often inadequate and superficial, leaving participants dissatisfied and cynical, and contribute little to teachers' learning and development (Armour and Yelling, 2004; Wright et al., 2008; Atencio et al., 2009).

If overall CPD for primary Physical Education falls short of demonstrating characteristics associated with effective provision, collective findings suggest that solutions should be built around the following five points ((NFER) 2001; (NPEAT) 1998; Ofsted 2002; O'Sullivan and Deglau, 2006; Pritchard and Marshall, 2002):

- the content is challenging, up-to-date and relevant to classroom practice;
- the activities are delivered with appropriate expertise;
- the activities are situated within the context of the school and its community;
- schools allow enough time to support effective professional development;
- teachers have access to follow-up sustained learning opportunities.

In order to do deliver on these points many schools will need to radically alter their structures, processes and priorities to enable CPD for primary Physical Education to happen effectively (Armour, 2006; Duncombe and Armour, 2004).

THOUGHT BOX

How useful has your own CPD experience been in primary Physical Education? How many of the five points recommended above relate to your own CPD experience?

Conclusion

The disconnections and weaknesses evident in training, practice and CPD are many and complex and what is evident is that devoting less time, little expertise and few resources in any package will not adequately address the issue. As Harris et al. (2012) note, these weaknesses need to be addressed through a dual approach of 'sufficient' PE-ITT followed by 'effective' PE-CPD which engages teachers and their colleagues in long-term collaborative endeavours that support transformative practice. Measures to be taken would include a clear understanding of the curriculum, appropriate ITE, personalised professional development, managing subject support within a professional learning community and effective subject leadership (Keay and Spence, 2012).

Further to this, at the teacher education level, movement towards a profession which develops a pedagogical expertise necessitates students to engage in two key processes. First, a narrative retrospection of student perceptions about schooling, sports and Physical Education, in which existing and changing beliefs and values become the centre of an examination of the wider movement culture as a basis of Physical Education; and second, learning to teach is organised through a process of observation, evaluation, planning and teaching that involves a continual cycle of switching from theory to teaching and back again. At the forefront of these processes partners within teacher education must work to achieve a conceptual agreement which develops compatible ideologies of teaching-learning within Physical Education based upon a 'leitmotiv of learning to reflect' (Crum, 1993: 352). To achieve such lofty ambitions, those within schools and universities need to recognise that the relationship between beliefs, learning and change is not a sequential process (Opfer et al., 2010). Assuming that belief change leads to practice change or vice versa oversimplifies a complex processes and isolating these elements ignores their entangled existence within the process of teachers' learning (Opfer et al., 2010). By conceptualising Physical Education as a 'collaborative endeavour' that involves 'complex interactions amongst and between children, teachers, head teachers, local authority managers and policy makers' Atencio et al. (2009: 1) argue learning becomes a product of the changing relationships between these groups of stakeholders. Professional development which will lead to change in practice must be rooted in collaborative and reflective professional learning environments that put the experiences and needs of teachers at the centre of learning. Consequently, continuing professional development programmes must become decentralised and adopt flexible structures, encouraging 'reflection and action' (Billet, 2001) or pedagogical support which is 'intensive, on-going and connected to practice' (Darling-Hammond et al., 2009). By analysing the relationships between beliefs, practices and knowledge sources, teachers should be supported in reflecting upon the existing structure of their pedagogical content knowledge and be encouraged to make connections within this knowledge. Most importantly accompanying experimentation with these differing pedagogical approaches will be the need to broaden and deepen subject knowledge (Ward, 2011).

KEY READINGS

A broad overview of both key issues and recommendations regarding primary Physical Education teacher training can be found in Keay, J. and Spence, J. (2012) Addressing training and development needs in primary Physical Education, in G. Griggs (ed.) (2012) *An Introduction to Primary Physical Education* (London: Routledge). A seminal paper exploring Physical Education CPD should also be examined and thus see, Armour, K. and Yelling, M. (2004) Continuing professional development for experienced physical education teachers: towards effective provision, *Sport, Education and Society*, 9(1), 95–114. For contemporary work bringing many of these key issues together, which includes an empirical focus, look no further than Harris, J., Cale, L. and Musson, H. (2012): The predicament of primary physical education: a consequence of 'insufficient' ITT and 'ineffective' CPD?, *Physical Education and Sport Pedagogy*, 17(4), 367–381.

References

Alexander, R. (2008) Pedagogy, curriculum and practice. In K. Hall, P. Murphy and J. Soler, (eds) *Pedagogy and Practice: Culture and Identities*. Milton Keynes: Open University Press,.

Armour, K. (2006) Physical education teachers as career-long learners: a compelling research agenda, *Physical Education and Sport Pedagogy*, 11, 203–7.

Armour, K.M. and Yelling, M. (2002) 'Talk and chalk' or learning from 'doing': continuing professional development for physical education teachers, *British Journal of Teaching Physical Education*, 33, 40–42.

Armour, K.M. and Yelling, M.R. (2004) Continuing professional development for experienced physical education teachers: towards effective provision, *Sport, Education and Society*, 9(1), 95–114.

Atencio, M., Jess, M. and Dewar, K. (2009). It is a case of changing your thought processes, the way you actually teach: implementing a complex professional learning agenda in Scottish Physical Education, paper presented at the British Educational Research Association Annual Conference, University of Manchester, 2–5 September 2009.

Billett, S. (2001) Learning thorough working life: interdependencies at work, *Studies in Continuing Education*, 23(1), 19–35.

Blair, R. and Capel, S. (2008) Intended or unintended? Issues arising from the implementation of the UK Government's 2003 Schools Workforce Remodelling Act, *Perspectives in Education*, 26(2), 105–121.

Blair, R. and Capel, S. (2011) Primary physical education, coaches and continuing professional development, *Sport, Education and Society*, 16(4), 485–505.

British Council for Physical Education (BCPE) (1980) *Policy statement*. London: BCPE.

Burgess, H. (2000) What future for initial teacher education? New curriculum and new directions, *Curriculum Journal*, 11(3), 405–417.

Caldecott, S., Warburton, P. and Waring, M. (2006a) A survey of the time devoted to the preparation of primary and junior school trainee teachers to teach physical education in England, *British Journal of Teaching Physical Education*, 37, 45–48.

Caldecott, S., Warburton, P. and Waring, M. (2006b) A survey of the time devoted to the preparation of primary and junior school trainee teachers to teach physical education in England (Part Two), *Physical Education Matters*, 1, 45–48.

Capel, S. (2007) Moving beyond physical education subject knowledge to develop knowledgeable teachers of the subject, *Curriculum Journal*, 18(4), 493–507.

Capel, S. and Katene, W. (2000) Secondary PGCE PE students' perceptions of their subject knowledge, *European Physical Education Review*, 6(1), 46–70.

Capel, S., Hayes, S., Katene, W. and Velija, P. (2009) The development of knowledge for teaching physical education in secondary schools over the course of a PGCE year, *European Journal of Teacher Education*, 32(1), 51–62.

Carney, C. and Armstrong, N. (1996) The provision of physical education in primary initial teacher training courses in England and Wales, *European Physical Education Review*, 2, 64–74.

Central Council for Physical Recreation (CCPR) (2004) *CCPR challenge 2004–2005*. London: CCPR.

Central Council for Physical Recreation (CCPR) and National Association of Head Teachers (NAHT) (1992) *National survey of physical education in primary schools. A sporting chance?* London: CCPR/NAHT.

Clay, G. (1999) 'Movement' – backwards and forwards: The influence of government on physical education – an HMI perspective, *British Journal of Physical Education*, 30, 38–41.

Crum, B. (1993) Conventional thought and practice in Physical Education: problems of teaching and implications for change, *Quest*, 45, 339–356.

Curtner-Smith, M.D. (1997) The impact of biography, teacher education, and organisational socialisation on the perspectives of first-year physical education teachers. Case studies of recruits with coaching orientations, *Sport, Education and Society*, 2(1), 73–94.

Curtner-Smith, M.D. (1999) The more things change the more they stay the same: factors influencing teachers' interpretations and delivery of National Curriculum Physical Education, *Sport, Education and Society*, 4(1), 75–97.

Curtner-Smith, M.D., Hastie, P.A. and Kinchin, G.D. (2008) Influence of occupational socialization on beginning teachers' interpretation and delivery of Sport Education, *Sport, Education and Society*, 13(9), 7–117.

Darling-Hammond, L. (2000) How teacher education matters, *Journal of Teacher Education*, 51(3), 166–173.

Darling-Hammond, L., Chung Wei, R., Andree, A., Richardson, N. and Orphanos, S. (2009) Professional learning in the learning profession: a status report on teacher development in the United States and abroad. Available online at www.nsdc.org/news/NSDCstudy2009.pdf (accessed 8 September 2011).

Davies, H.J. (1999) Standards in physical education in England at key stage 1 and key stage 2: past, present and future, *European Review of Physical Education*, 4, 173–188.

DeCorby, K., Halas, J., Dixon, S., Wintrup, L. and Janzen, H. (2005) Classroom teachers and the challenges of delivering quality physical education, *Journal of Educational Research*, 98(4), 208–220.

Department for Education (DfE) (1992) *Department for Education Circular 9/92: New Requirements for Initial Teacher Training*. London: HMSO.

Department for Education and Skills (DfES) and Department for Culture, Media and Sport (DCMS) (2003) *Learning Through PE and Sport: A Guide to the Physical Education, School Sport and Club Links Strategy*. Annesley: DfES Publications.

Department for Education and Skills (DfES) and the Qualifications and Curriculum Authority (QCA) (1999) *Physical education. The national curriculum for England. Key stages 1–4*. London: HMSO.

Doolittle, S.A., Dodds, P. and Placek, J.H. (1993) Persistence of beliefs about teaching during formal training of preservice teachers, *Journal of Teaching in Physical Education*, 12, 355–365.

Downey, J. (1979) The training in physical education of the non-specialist primary school teacher, *Bulletin of Physical Education*, 15, 5–10.

Duncombe, R. and Armour, K. (2004) Collaborative professional learning: from theory to practice, *Journal of In-service Education*, 30, 141–166.

Duncombe, R. and Armour, K. (2005) The school as a community of practice for primary physical education: The myths and the reality. Paper presented at the British Educational Research Association Annual Conference, 15–17 September, at the University of Glamorgan, Wales.

Evans, J.B., Davies, B. and Penney, D. (1996) Teachers, teaching and the social construction of gender relations, *Sport, Education and Society*, 1(2), 165–183.

Giroux, H. (2009) Teachers as transformatory intellectuals. In K. Ryan and J. Cooper (eds) *Kaleidoscope Contemporary and Classical Readings in Education*. Belmont, CA: Wadsworth CENGAGE Learning.

Graves, T. (2008) 'TOPS' view: implementation and evaluation in Hertfordshire, *Primary PE Focus*, 208, 17–19.

Green, K. (1998) Philosophies, ideologies and the practice of physical education, *Sport, Education and Society*, 3(2), 125–143.

Green, K. (2008) *Understanding Physical Education*. London: Sage.

Griggs, G. (2008) Outsiders inside: The use of sports coaches in primary schools in the West Midlands. *Physical Education Matters*, 3(2), 33–6.

Griggs, G. (2010) For sale – primary Physical Education. £20 per hour or nearest offer, *Education 3–13*, 38(1), 39–46.

Hardman, K. and Marshall, J. (2005) Physical education in schools in European context: charter principles, promises and implementation realities. In K. Green and K. Hardman (eds) *Physical Education*. London: Sage.

Hardy, C. (1999) Preservice teachers' perceptions of learning to teach in a predominantly school-based teacher education program, *Journal of Teaching Physical Education*, 18(2), 175–198.

Harris, J., Cale, L. and Musson, H. (2012) The predicament of primary physical education: a consequence of 'insufficient' ITT and 'ineffective' CPD?, *Physical Education and Sport Pedagogy*, 17(4), 367–381.

Haskins, D. (2003) *TOP Play and TOP Sport Handbook*. Loughborough, UK: Youth Sport Trust.

Haydn-Davies, D. (2008) What do we need to know about as teachers of Primary Physical Education? Big benefits from working with little learners, *Primary Physical Education Matters*, 3(2), v–vi.

Haydn-Davies, D. and Spence, J. (2010) The importance of goats in primary initial teacher education: a case study in Physical Education. Paper presented at the British Educational Research Association Annual Conference, Warwick University, September 2010.

Hobson, A.J. (2002) Student teachers' perceptions of school-based mentoring in initial teacher training, *Mentoring and Tutoring*, 10(1), 5–20.

Hunt, M. (1998) TOP play BT TOP sport: an effective influence on teaching?, *Bulletin of Physical Education*, 34, 194–205.

Keay, J. and Spence, J. (2012) Addressing training and development needs in primary Physical Education. In G. Griggs (ed.) *An Introduction to Primary Physical Education*. London: Routledge.

Kerr, J.H. and Rodgers, M. (1981) Primary school physical education: non-specialist teacher preparation and attitudes, *Bulletin of Physical Education*, 17, 13–20.

Kirk, D. (2010) *Physical Education Futures*. London: Routledge.

Lawrence, J. (2003) The impact and use of the TOPs programme in one local education authority, *British Journal of Teaching Physical Education*, 34, 44–48.

Lawson, H.A. (1983a) Toward a model of teacher socialisation in physical education: the subjective warrant, recruitment and teacher education (Part 1), *Journal of Teaching in Physical Education*, 2(3), 3–16.

Lawson, H.A. (1983b) Toward a model of teacher socialisation in physical education: entry into schools, teachers' role orientations and longevity in teaching (Part 2), *Journal of Teaching in Physical Education*, 3(1), 3–15.

Morgan, I. (1997) The preparation of physical education teachers during initial teacher training, *British Journal of Physical Education*, 28, 18–20.

Morgan, P. and Bourke, M. (2005) An investigation of pre-service and primary school teacher perspectives of PE teaching confidence and PE teacher education, *ACHPER Healthy Lifestyles Journal*, 52(1), 7–13.

Morgan, P. and Bourke, S. (2008) Non-specialist teachers' confidence to teach PE: the nature and influence of personal experiences in schools, *Physical Education and Sport Pedagogy*, 13(1), 1–29.

National Association of Head Teachers (NAHT) (1999) Survey of physical education and sports in schools, *British Journal of Physical Education*, 30, 29–31.

National Foundation for Educational Research (NFER) (2001) Continuing professional development: LEA and school support for teachers. Slough, UK: NFER.

National Partnership for Excellence and Accountability in Teaching (NPEAT) (1998) Improving professional development: eight research-based principles. Available online at http://www.smsu.edu/graduatestudies/ed/npeat%20prof%20dev.pdf (accessed 8 September 2011).

Office for Standards in Education (Ofsted) (1998) *Teaching Physical Education in the Primary School: The Initial Training of Teachers*. London: HMSO.

Office for Standards in Education (Ofsted) (2000) *Annual Report of Her Majesty's Chief Inspector of Schools, 1998–99*. London: HMSO.

Office for Standards in Education (Ofsted) (2002) *Continuing Professional Development for Teachers in Schools*. HMI 410. London: HMSO.

Office for Standards in Education Ofsted (Ofsted) (2004) *Physical Education in Secondary Schools*. London: TSO.

Office for Standards in Education (Ofsted) (2005) *Physical Education in Primary Schools*. London: TSO.

Office for Standards in Education (Ofsted) (2009) *Physical Education in Primary Schools (2005–2008)*. London: TSO.

Opfer, D.V., Pedder, D.G. and Lavicza, Z. (2010). The role of teachers' orientation to learning in professional development and change: a national study of teachers in England, *Teaching and Teacher Education*, 27(2), 443–543.

O'Sullivan, M. and Deglau, D. (2006) Principles of professional development, *Journal of Teaching in Physical Education*, 25, 441–449.

Physical Education Association of the United Kingdom (PEA UK) (1984) *Professional courses in Physical Education for non-specialist primary and middle school teachers, 1977–1983*. London: PEA UK.

Physical Education Association of the United Kingdom (PEA UK) (1987) *Report of a commission of enquiry: Physical Education in schools*. London: PEA UK.

Pickup, I. (2006) Telling tales from school: trainee primary teachers' experiences in physical education. Paper presented at the British Education Research Association Annual Conference, 6–9 September, in Warwick, UK.

Placek, J.H. (1983) Conceptions of success in teaching: busy, happy, and good? In T. Templin and J. Olsen (eds) *Teaching in Physical Education*. Champaign, IL: Human Kinetics Publishers.

Pritchard, R.J. and Marshall, J.C. (2002) Professional development in 'healthy' vs. 'unhealthy' districts: top ten characteristics based on research, *School Leadership and Management*, 22, 113–141.

Roberts, D., Leach, R., Harries, J., Phillips, R.W., Newton, H.R. and Jones, S. (1998) TOP play and BT TOP sport in the North West, *Bulletin of Physical Education*, 34, 134–145.

Rolfe, L. (2001) The factors which influence primary student teachers' confidence to teach dance, *European Physical Education Review*, 7, 157–175.

Rolfe, L. and Chedzoy, S. (1997) Student teachers' perceptions of teaching dance in primary schools, *European Journal of Physical Education*, 2, 218–227.

Rossi, T. and Cassidy, T. (1999). Knowledgeable teachers in Physical Education: a view of teachers' knowledge. In C. Hardy and M. Mawer (eds) *Learning and Teaching in Physical Education*. Lewes: Falmer Press.

Smyth, D. (1995) First-year physical education teachers' perceptions of their workplace, *Journal of Teaching in Physical Education*, 14(2), 198–214.

Solmon, M.A. and Ashy, M.H. (1995) Value orientations of pre-service teachers, *Research Quarterly for Exercise and Sport*, 66, 219–230.

Sparks, D. (2002) Designing powerful professional development for teachers and principals. Available online at http://www.friscoisd.org/ly/departments/professionalDev/documents/DesigningPowerfulProfessionalDevelopmentforTeachersand Principals_000.pdf (accessed 2 December 2014).

Spode, I. (1997) An evaluative case study into the effect 'TOP Play' and 'TOP Sport' has had on the quality of teaching and pupil responses within eight primary schools, *Bulletin of Physical Education*, 33, 42–49.

Sport England (2002) *Sport and education. Sport England briefing note*. London: Sport England.

Sport England (2005) *Planning, preparation and assessment time for primary school teachers. Briefing note*. Ilkeston: Vaga Associates.

Standing Conference on Physical Education (SCOPE) (1991) Survey of initial teacher training – 1990/1991. Unpublished report. London: SCOPE.

Stroot, S.A. and Ko, B. (2006). Induction of beginning physical educators into the school setting. In D. Kirk, D. Macdonald and M. O'Sullivan (eds) *The Handbook of Physical Education*. London: Sage Publications.

Times Educational Supplement/Central Council for Physical Recreation (2003) Pupils fail swimming test, *Times Educational Supplement*, 1 August, 27.

Tinning, R. (2006). Theoretical orientations in physical education teacher education. In D. Kirk, D. Macdonald and M. O'Sullivan (eds) *The Handbook of Physical Education*. London: Sage Publications.

Training Development Agency for schools (TDA) (2008) *Professional Standards for Qualified Teacher Status and Requirements for Initial Teacher Training (Revised 2008)*. London: TDA.

Tsangaridou, N. (2006) Teachers' beliefs. In D. Kirk, D. Macdonald and M. O'Sullivan (eds) *The Handbook of Physical Education*. London: Sage.

Warburton, P. (2001) A sporting future for all: Fact or fiction? *British Journal of Teaching Physical Education,* 32(2), 18–21.

Ward, G. (2011) Examining primary school Physical Education coordinators' pedagogical content knowledge of games: simply playing?, *Education 3–13*, 41(6), 562–585.

Wetz, J. (2010) *Is Initial Teacher Training Failing to Meet the Needs of All Our Young People?* Reading: CfBT Education Trust.

Williams, E.A. (1985) Perspectives on initial teacher training in physical education for primary school teachers. In *28th ICHPER World Congress Proceedings, Physical Education Association of Great Britain and Northern Ireland, and International Council on Health, Physical Education and Recreation* (pp. 726–734). London: West London Institute of Higher Education.

Williams, J. and Williamson, K.M. (1995) *Beginning to Teach Physical Education: The Inside Stories*. Dubuque, IA: Kendal/Hunt Publishing.

Williams, J. and Williamson, K.M. (1998) The socialisation strategies of first-year physical education teachers: conflicts and concessions, *Physical Educator*, 55(2), 78–88.

Woodhouse, J. (2006) Induction support in physical education and school sport for newly qualified primary generalist teachers. Unpublished report. Reading, UK: Association for Physical Education.

Wright, L. (2002) Rescuing primary physical education and saving those values that matter most, *British Journal of Teaching Physical Education*, 33, 37–39.

Wright, J., Konza, D., Hearne, D. and Okely, T. (2008) The Gold Medal Fitness Program: a model for teacher change, *Physical Education and Sport Pedagogy*, 13(1), 49–64.

Youth Sport Trust (YST) (1997) *Annual Report, 1996–1997*. London: YST.

5

TEACHING PRIMARY PHYSICAL EDUCATION

Introduction

Penney and Waring (2000: 6) indicate that much of the practice of Physical Education is too focused on the detailed *content* of what is to be taught – e.g. how to bowl overarm in cricket rather on the ways it might be taught. For effective Physical Education to take place it is the relationship between the trinity of *what* to teach, *how* to teach and *why* to teach it that should become the most important consideration. A useful tool to provide further insights into this area has been the framework proposed by Shulman (1987), which uses the concept of a teachers' pedagogical content knowledge (PCK). PCK is a knowledge that cannot be acquired through simply reading a book but rather it is developed over a long period of time through reflecting on practice (Amade-Escot, 2000). Therefore in its entirety 'a teacher's PCK represents the integration of different forms of knowledge, experiences, beliefs and values' (Ward, 2012: 3) and comprises the following areas (Shulman, 1987):

a   knowledge of the subject or content;
b   general pedagogical knowledge;
c   curricular knowledge;
d   pedagogical content knowledge;
e   knowledge of learners;
f   knowledge of contexts;
g   knowledge of the purposes of teaching.

Application of this framework in researching Physical Education teachers has highlighted the complex relationships that exist between these different knowledge bases and how they impact upon the selection and presentation of the subject matter and the pedagogical strategies they employ (Grossman, 1989; Amade-Escot, 2000; Rovegno, 2003; Ward, 2012).

Veal and MaKinster (1999) further consider the hierarchical relationships that exist within and between the various components of teachers' PCK. In their stratified model PCK is examined at three levels: general PCK (e.g. Physical Education), domain-specific PCK (e.g. activity areas such as Games) and topic-specific PCK (e.g. a net wall game such as tennis and its related content). Analysis in this way can reveal greater detail in the characteristics of a teacher's PCK and indicate how they may seek connections within and between the different levels of their PCK. For example, a teacher may have a well-developed philosophy of Physical Education and broad knowledge or wider pedagogical strategies located at the general PCK level. However lower down at the domain and topic-specific level, their knowledge maybe limited restricting the relationship between the levels and then limiting the resulting practice (Rovegno, 2003). More recent research conducted by Ward (2012) illustrates the point perfectly whereby teachers placed a misplaced emphasis on topic specific PCK such as skills to use in netball and consequently were wedded to delivering them using a narrow range of pedagogic practice akin to sports coaching.

> Their preoccupation with developing competence in sporting forms of games, allied to the very narrow success criteria of enjoyment and participation, created problems in providing authentic, differentiated learning experiences. The absence of knowledge drawn from other pedagogical strategies, which may have been used in other subjects and domains to create dofferentiated learning experiences, points towards a significant compartmentalisation of their domain-specific PCK of games.
>
> (Ward, 2012: 16)

What becomes of interest more broadly therefore is the pedagogical approach that they might take and how this impacts upon teaching and learning experience.

Understanding teaching and learning

Mosston and Ashworth's Spectrum of Teaching Styles (Mosston and Ashworth, 2002) provide a very useful way of viewing and understanding fundamental ideas about both teaching and learning in Physical Education. The eleven teaching styles identified, denoted by a letter in the original text, are shown in Box 5.1 that follows with a brief explanation concerning both the role of the teacher and the learner.

Mosston and Ashworth (2002) indicate that the earlier the letter in the alphabet, the more direct the teaching is, typical of teachers who wish to have complete control of information, resources and learner behaviour. These earlier letters are referred to as being 'reproductive' practices as they require nothing more from the learner than the reproduction of the information given to them by

BOX 5.1 SUMMARY OF MOSSTON AND ASHWORTH'S (2002) SPECTRUM OF TEACHING STYLES

A Command

In this style the teacher tells the learners what to do and makes all the decisions. Learners are expected to copy and comply with the instructions given.

B Practice

Here the teacher sets up practices or drills for the learners to engage with. Learners must establish what is required of them and then typically repeat actions with the aim of improving. The teacher may also provide a role of giving feedback during the activity.

C Reciprocal

In this style learners work together and receive feedback from each other during a given task. While the learners are performing and assessing each other, again the teacher provides feedback, either directly or indirectly.

D Self-check

The teacher sets a task and sets accompanying criteria to determine success. Learners are required to check their own performance against these criteria.

E Inclusion

Here the teacher sets out a variety of tasks, typically in a circuit or carousel type arrangement. Learners can either select a task which they feel is appropriate or complete all tasks to their own motivation or ability.

F Guided discovery

In this style the teacher uses questions during tasks to direct learners towards a pre-determined outcome.

G Convergent discovery

The teacher sets a problem and the learner attempts to find the most appropriate solution again focused towards a pre-determined outcome.

H Divergent discovery

The teacher sets a problem and the learner attempts to find the most appropriate solution though the outcome is open and not pre-determined.

I Learner designed

Here the teacher decides on a topic to focus upon and the learners develop activities themselves within this area, drawing on the teachers' expertise when required.

J Learner initiated

The learner decides what they are aiming to achieve and the teacher supports them in this pursuit as needed.

K Self-teach

Here the learner engages in their own development without the need of the teacher.

the teacher. As indicated in Chapter 2, reproductive practices have proved very resilient to change (Tsangaridou, 2006) and consequently Physical Education practice continues to be delivered using a limited range of teaching approaches, the most prevalent of which are the didactic and teacher centred indicated by the earlier letters of the alphabet (Kirk, 2010). Though it is easy to be dismissive of such practices if a teacher's personal philosophies are located at the other end of the spectrum, there are good reasons why reproductive practices have become predominant.

A belief that a behaviourist approach to teaching and learning was the most effective was the dominant view of the first half of the twentieth century (Harris, 2000). In this mode little or no consideration is made of what happens in the mind of the learner and as such the teacher decides what knowledge is important and transmits it in a direct way to the learner (Chambers, 2011). Consequently a behaviourist approach has long held currency in Physical Education (Jess, 2011). However, as indicated by Light (2008: 22), 'although physical education teachers may not necessarily articulate clear beliefs about it, their practice invariably rests upon basic, unquestioned beliefs about learning… and that assume it to be an explicit linear and measurable process of internalising knowledge.' Though such beliefs originated in Psychology and permeated into other spheres such as

THOUGHT BOX

Reflect upon the Spectrum of Teaching Styles and consider which ones you employ. Due you use some more than others? When and why do you use them? Are there styles you never use? Perhaps you might consider giving a new one a try.

education, it is arguably Physical Education association with sport that has been responsible for its dependence on behaviourist approaches (Capel, 2000).

Within UK movement culture 'sport' has occupied a dominant position, traditionally conceived of as highly competitive in which the achievement motive has remained uppermost (Griggs and Ward, 2012) (see Chapter 2). As a consequence, pedagogically, a skills focused approach of 'physical education as sport techniques' has been pervasive for generations within both coaching and teaching structures (Kirk, 2011) (see Chapter 3). This has also been formally reinforced by placing the original key value of the National Curriculum for Physical Education on 'performance' (DES, 1991) and highly recommending a teaching model which comprised a structure of 'warm up, skill learning and a game or activity' (NCC, 1992). The emphasis on 'skill' development continues into the current programme of study for Physical Education in primary schools.

The difficulties in teacher training within Physical Education identified in Chapter 4 have also served to perpetuate a system where emphasis is placed on providing lessons within a curriculum in which children are being 'busy, happy, and good' (Placek, 1983) but with very little or no consideration of theoretical underpinning concerning the activities provided (Tinning, 2006) leading to what Light (2008: 26) refers to as 'Cognitive Dissonance'. This aspect has yet to be addressed satisfactorily within teacher training providers (Ward and Griggs, 2011).

Addressing cognitive dissonance: moving towards models-based practice

Within recent decades Physical Education practitioners involved in developing research in the subject have sought ways to address the apparent cognitive dissonance between theory and practice. The most significant development in this area has been the continuing interest in models based practice, where a model or series of models are used to deliver Physical Education lessons. These have been referred to as both 'pedagogical models' (Kirk, 2006) and 'instructional models' (Metzler, 2005) and can be explained as follows:

> An instructional model can be described as a comprehensive and coherent plan for teaching that includes a theoretical foundation, a statement of intended outcomes, teacher's content knowledge expertise, developmentally appropriate and sequenced learning activities, expectations for teacher and student behaviours, unique task structures, measures of learning outcomes and mechanisms for measuring the faithful implementation of the model itself.
>
> (Metzler, 2005: 16)

Metzler (2005) indicates that in order for Physical Education practitioners to provide experiences that purposefully contribute to all learning domains consideration needs to be given to not only the process of learning but different instructional methods, learning environments and learning theories. Put simply, the teacher must consider *how* to teach in addition to *what* to teach. The most influential factor may then become the selected instructional model rather than content as has been historically the case with Physical Education professionals (Penney, 1999).

The most well known of these in both research articles and in practice are Co-operative Learning, Sport Education and Teaching Games for Understanding (see Dyson et al., 2004).

Cooperative Learning (CL) is an instructional model that shifts the focus of learning to the student. A primary goal in CL is that each student becomes a meaningful participant in learning. Students work together in small, structured, heterogeneous groups to master the content. The students are not only responsible for learning the material, but also for helping their group-mates learn (Antil et al., 1998; Putnam, 1998).

Sport Education (SE) is a curriculum and instruction model designed to provide authentic, educationally rich sport experiences which links Physical Education to the wider sporting culture and aims to create competent, literate, and enthusiastic sports players (Siedentop, 2002). SE places students in small-sided teams and takes them through a series of skill practices and through developmentally appropriate games conducted as authentic competition. Students in sport education become members of teams that stay together for the entire length of a season (Siedentop, 1994).

Bunker and Thorpe (1982) developed the 'Teaching Games for Understanding' (TGfU) model, which highlights the motivational aspect for learners of playing games rather than the traditional practising of skills. Games are considered the ideal context in which to develop skills and can be conditioned to highlight specific tactical situations. Therefore, the playing of games becomes the main focus of learning; more specifically the promotion of tactical awareness and decision making is encouraged.

To date most research and practice concerning instructional models as been located at secondary school level, though there are some lesser-known exceptions. At a similar time to the development of TGfU, Mauldon and Redfern (1981) proposed a model for teaching games across the age range that encouraged the use of a problem solving approach. By utilising game and skill categories, teachers are encouraged to draw connections through the use of

THOUGHT BOX

Trying a model-based approach can be an interesting and challenging experience for both teachers and learners but CL, SE and TGfU do need practice. Consider which one might work best in a primary setting and why?

scenarios to emphasise tactical situations. More recently, interest in instructional models has seen a revisiting of their appropriateness and application at primary level (examples of success here are reported in O'Donovan, 2011).

A movement trend down the spectrum?

Interest in instructional models is perhaps illustrative of a movement trend down the teaching and learning spectrum to a world that is more child-centred in nature perhaps as a reaction to the apparent never changing years of behaviourist driven reproductive practice. Further to this seems to be a desire to locate or situate learning in a real context. Siedentop's (1994; 2002) development of sport education is a very good illustration of this. It is perhaps obvious that within our lifelong engagement with physical activity it is likely that we might wish to assume a number of roles within a sporting context than mere elite performer. If we learn how to participate in an authentic environment our understanding is more connected, relevant and arguably portable to other times and places in our lives, thereby furthering our likelihood to engage in greater lifelong physical activity during our life course (Green, 2012).

The underpinning theory to this shift is located away from behaviourism and into the realms of constructivism. Here learners construct their own knowledge through interaction and engagement with their environment and do not have to remain passive and rely upon the teacher to give them all the information (Malone, 2003; Duncombe and Armour, 2004). By engaging in learning in this way it is thought that learners engage in more critical thinking and become more adept at solving problems (Sewell, 2002). The skill in this approach from a teacher's perspective is as they move down the alphabet of the teaching and learning spectrum – e.g. to F (guided discovery) or G (convergent learning) – that they can adapt their role to something closer to that of a facilitator rather than an instructor which they may have been used to. Uncertainty here for the inexperienced or insecure rests in the self doubt that ensues when they are not in complete command of either the content or the behaviour in a way they had become accustomed.

How far down the spectrum do we stray?

An interesting paradox exists whereby it is well known that teaching and learning experiences have been dominated by didactic approaches to delivery and yet there remains a literature that continues to celebrate Physical Education's ability to offer opportunities to make choices and engage in episodes of discovery (Chedzoy, 2006; QCA, 2007). As with instructional models, a closer examination of the pedagogic examples given in guidance for practitioners indicate the use of either F (guided discovery) or G (convergent learning) as a preferred pedagogical approach, which by the end of the lesson are designed to lead pupils to a planned, predetermined response (Katone, 1949). 'This structure gets the learner to the target with maximum efficiency' (Mosston and Ashworth, 2002: 220) and is consistent with performativity discourses which specify both objectives and outcomes and is the basis for much of the structure found in QCA planning (QCA, 2000), prevalent in planning for primary school Physical Education. As a method of discovery, however, this approach has its limits, not least because cognitively it is still reproductive in nature (Bruner, 1961). Indeed research in primary education by both Alexander (2004) and Moyles et al. (2003) found that dominant pedagogical strategies have reduced teacher–pupil interaction to be 'dominated by closed questions, brief answers which teachers do not build upon' (Alexander, 2004: 21).

With an endless range of movement possibilities that can be combined and recombined it might be that unlocking this potential requires the right tool. One possible solution is to employ the H divergent discovery approach where the learner makes most of the key decisions and is engaged cognitively throughout in a process of designing and evaluation. According to Mosston and Ashworth (2002: 248), 'without experiences in divergent discovery, learners' experiences are limited to replication of the known movements, basic skills and fundamental strategies in the different activities and sports'. To employ this approach successfully a less constrained learning environment and the use of precise language are key. For example, gymnastic sequencing must go beyond the practice pedagogy and vocabulary of 'show or find three ways to ...' to a more open 'create five different movements from a stimulus and connect using ...' where the teacher merely specifies guiding parameters (Griggs, 2009).

The impact of policy and fashion on teaching and learning experiences

As indicated in earlier chapters, policy initiatives over the last two decades have resulted in a low level of teacher confidence in delivering Physical Education (DeCorby et al., 2005; Morgan and Bourke, 2005, 2008). As also discussed has been the resulting willingness of primary staff to wish to give up teaching Physical Education and buy in inexpensive non-QTS personnel, in particular sports coaches, to deliver these lessons (Griggs, 2010; Blair and Capel, 2011). However what both groups (unconfident teachers and coaches) have in common is that they often remain unsure about what activities are suitable for primary-aged children, especially in Key Stage 1. A fashion that has filled this void has been packages that have focused on what have been termed fundamentals, fundamental movements, fundamental movement skills or FMS, consisting of basic locomotor, manipulative and balance skills.

Locomotor skills refer to a body moving from one point to another. Activities such as walking, running, jumping, hopping, skipping, galloping, sliding, leaping and climbing are representative examples of locomotor movement skills (Gallahue and Cleland-Donnelly, 2007). Manipulative skills include either gross motor or fine motor movements. Gross motor manipulative skills involve movements that give force to objects or receive force from objects. Throwing, catching, kicking, trapping, striking, volleying, bouncing, rolling and punting are examples of fundamental gross motor manipulative skills. Fine motor manipulative skills refer to small object-handling activities that emphasise motor control, precision and accuracy of movement. Balance refers to both the body remaining in place but moving around its horizontal or vertical axis (Gallahue and Cleland-Donnelly, 2007) and the process for maintaining postural stability (Westcott et al., 1997). More specifically, Westcott et al. defined static balance as 'the ability to maintain a posture, such as balancing in a standing or sitting position', and dynamic balance as 'the ability to maintain postural control during other movements, such as reaching for an object or walking across a lawn' (630). According to Gallahue and Cleland-Donnelly (2007), axial movements, such as bending, stretching, twisting, turning, swinging, body inversion, body rolling, and landing/stopping are all considered as balance skills.

Keen to get business, a range of companies have wrapped and rewrapped different lists of these movements that children should undertake in order to provide secure movement foundations. Some papers have suggested that the adoption of these programmes facilitates participation and success in many sport and exercise activities undertaken during school and leisure time (Barnett et al., 2008). Others have gone further indicating that engagement with FMS will improve chances of continued lifelong physical activity (Stodden et al., 2008; Haywood and Getchell, 2009). Though there are, of course, merits in such programmes, as children do need secure movement foundations, serious questions remain. For example, how much evidence is there about these programmes to merit widescale adoption? One need only look at the lack of evidence base, yet widescale adoption of combined physical and cognitive exercises that swept the UK in the void before FMS to put this latest fashion into context.

Conclusion

When one reflects upon the trinity outlined in the introduction if teachers and coaches flit between *what* to teach or use packaged content 'off the peg' and do not understand *why* they are teaching it then we quickly revert to busy, happy and good lessons with continuing cognitive dissonance. Furthermore, the widescale adoption of fundamental movement type approaches appears to direct *how* primary Physical Education is taught back up the Spectrum of Teaching Styles towards A (Command) and B (Practice styles).

Recent research projects such as that carried out by Spence and Haydn-Davies (2011) have asked teachers about these issues and the barriers they face in being able to deliver quality Physical Education, with the results being very illuminating. Findings highlighted a lack of confidence in teaching Physical Education, with staff reporting insufficient knowledge of how to develop children's physical skills with many feeling that they lacked an understanding of what children should be able to do at different stages and how to set appropriate activities which would help children learn and develop. The teachers also highlighted that they lacked confidence in assessment and had difficulty in recording assessments and possessed a lack of techniques about how to do this. The simple truth is that if primary Physical Education is to move on the basics of a planning, teaching and assessment have got to be in place. This needs to feature in teacher training, be evident in the classroom and be a strong feature of CPD programmes. If this remains unaddressed we must resign primary Physical Education to a future of unassessed, busy, happy and good sessions where children are occupied and 'babysat' and where learning is forgotten.

KEY READINGS

Getting to grips with teaching styles is a useful exercise so going through each of them step by step is essential – see Mosston, M. and Ashworth, S. (2002) *Teaching Physical Education* (5th edition; London: Pearson Education). Equally valuable is developing an understanding for the different approaches that have been taken to underpin and justify teaching and learning experiences in physical education. An excellent summary can be found in Chambers, F. (2011) Learning Theory for effective learning in practice, in K. Armour (ed.) *Sport Pedagogy* (Harlow: Prentice Hall). Finally, to avoid cognitive dissonance, a useful overview of different models based approaches can be found in Dyson, B., Griffin, L. and Hastie, P. (2004) Sport education, tactical games, and cooperative learning: theoretical and pedagogical considerations, *Quest*, 56, 226–240.

References

Alexander, R. (2004) Still no pedagogy? Principle, pragmatism and compliance in primary education, *Cambridge Journal of Education*, 34(1), 7–33.

Amade-Escot, C. (2000) The contribution of two research programmes on teaching content: pedagogical content knowledge and didactics of physical education, *Journal of Teaching in Physical Education*, 20(1), 78–101.

Antil, L., Jenkins, J., Wayne, S. and Vadasy, P. (1998) Cooperative learning: prevalence, conceptualizations, and the relation between research and practice, *American Education Research Journal*, 35, 419.

Bailey, R., Armour, K., Kirk, D., Jess, M., Pickup, I., Sandford, R. and BERA Physical Education and Sport Pedagogy Special Interest Group. (2009) The educational benefits claimed for physical education and school sport: an academic review, *Research Papers in Education*, 24(1), 1–27.

Barnett, L.M., Morgan, P.J., van Beurden, E. and Beard, J.R. (2008) Perceived sports competence mediates the relationship between childhood motor skill proficiency and adolescent physical activity and fitness: a longitudinal assessment, *International Journal of Behavioral Nutrition and Physical Activity*, 5(1), 40.

Blair, R. and Capel, S. (2011) Primary physical education, coaches and continuing professional development, *Sport, Education and Society*, 16(4), 485–505.

Bloom, B.S. (ed.) (1956) *Taxonomy of Educational Objectives, Book 1, Cognitive Domain.* New York: David McKay.

Bruner, J.S. (1961) The act of discovery, *Harvard Educational Review*, 31, 21–32.

Bunker, D. and Thorpe, R. (1982) A model for the teaching of games in the secondary school, *Bulletin of Physical Education*, 18(1), 5–8.

Capel, S. (2000) Approaches to teaching games. In S. Capel and S. Piotrowski (eds) *Issues in Physical Education*. London: Routledge Falmer.

Capel, S. (2007) Moving beyond physical education subject knowledge to develop knowledgeable teachers of the subject, *Curriculum Journal*, 18(4), 493–507.

Chambers, F. (2011) Learning Theory for effective learning in practice. In K. Armour (ed.) *Sport Pedagogy*. Harlow: Prentice Hall.

Chedzoy, S. (2006) Children, creativity and Physical Education. Primary PE Matters, *Physical Education Matters*, 1(1), 4–5.

DeCorby, K., Halas, J., Dixon, S., Wintrup, L. and Janzen, H. (2005) Classroom teachers and the challenges of delivering quality physical education, *The Journal of Educational Research*, 98(4), 208–220.

Department of Education and Science (DES) (1991) *Physical Education for Age 5–16.* London: DES.

Duncombe, R. and Armour, K. (2004) Collaborative professional development learning: from theory to practice, *Journal of In-service Education*, 30, 141–166.

Dyson, B., Griffin, L. and Hastie, P. (2004) Sport education, tactical games, and cooperative learning: rheoretical and pedagogical considerations, *Quest*, 56, 226–40.

Evans, J., Davies, B. and Penney, D. (1996) Teachers, teaching and the social construction of gender relations, *Sport, Education and Society*, 1(2), 165–183.

Gallahue, D.L. and Cleland-Donnelly, F. (2007) *Developmental Physical Education for all Children*. Leeds: Human Kinetics.

Green, K. (2012): Mission impossible? Reflecting upon the relationship between physical education, youth sport and lifelong participation, *Sport, Education and Society*, 19(4), 357–375.

Griggs, G. (2009) 'What you risk reveals what you value': fostering creativity in primary Physical Education. *Education 3–13*, 37(2), 121–130.

Griggs, G. (2010) For sale – primary physical education. £20 per hour or nearest offer, *Education*, 3–13, 38(1), 39–46.

Griggs, G. and Ward, G. (2012) Physical Education in the UK: disconnections and reconnections, *Curriculum Journal*, 23(2), 207–229.

Grossman, P. (1989) A study of contrast: sources of pedagogical content knowledge for secondary English, *Journal of Teacher Education*, 40, 24–32.

Harris, J. (2000) Revisioning the boundaries of learning theory in the assessment of prior experiential learning (APEL), SCRUTEA, 30th annual conference, University of Nottingham.

Harrow, A.J. (1972) *A Taxonomy of the Psychomotor Domain*. New York: Longman.

Haywood, K.M. and Getchell, N. (2009) *Life Span Motor Development*. Leeds: Human Kinetics.

Jess, M. (2011) Becoming an effective primary school teacher. In K. Armour (ed.) *Sport Pedagogy*. Harlow: Prentice Hall.

Katone, G. (1949) *Organising and Memorising*. New York: Columbia University Press.

Kirk, D. (2006) The idea of Physical Education and its discontents. Inaugural lecture, Leeds Metropolitan University, 27 June 2006.

Kirk, D. (2010) *Physical Education Futures*. London: Routledge.

Kirk, D. (2011) The crisis of content knowledge: how PETE maintains the id² of physical education-as-sport-techniques (Part 3), *Physical Education Matters*, 6(2), 34–36.

Laker, A. (2000) *Beyond the Boundaries of Physical Education: Educating Young People for Citizenship and Social Responsibility*. London: Routledge/Falmer.

Light, R. (2008) 'Complex' learning theory in physical education: an examination of its epistemology and assumptions about how we learn, *Journal of Teaching in Physical Education*, 27(1), 21–37.

Malone, S. (2003) *Learning About Learning. An A–Z of Training and Development Tools and Techniques*. London: The Cromwell Press.

Mauldon, E. and Redfern, H. (1981) *Games Teaching: An Approach for the Primary School*. Plymouth: Macdonald and Evans.

Metzler, M.W. (2005) *Instructional Models for Physical Education*. Scottsdale, AZ: Holcomb Hathaway Publishers.

Morgan, P. and Bourke, S. (2005) An investigation of pre-service and primary school teachers' perspectives of Physical Education teaching confidence and Physical Education teacher education, *ACHPER Healthy Lifestyles Journal*, 52(1), 7–13.

Morgan, P. and Bourke, S. (2008) Non-specialist teachers' confidence to teach Physical Education: the nature and influence of personal school experiences in Physical Education, *Physical Education and Sport Pedagogy*, 13(1), 1–29.

Mosston, M. and Ashworth, S. (2002) *Teaching Physical Education* (5th edition). London: Pearson Education.

Moyles, J., Hargreaves, L., Merry, R., Paterson, F. and Esart-Sarries, V. (2003) *Interactive Teaching in the Primary School: Digging Deeper into Meanings*. Maidenhead: Open University Press.

National Curriculum Council (NCC) (1992) *Non-statutory Guidance for Physical Education*. London: HMSO.

O'Donovan, T. (2011) Models based practice: structuring teaching and coaching to meet learners' diverse needs. In K. Armour (ed.) *Sport Pedagogy*. Harlow: Prentice Hall.

Office for Standards in Education (2001) *Secondary Subject Reports 2000/01: Physical Education*. London: HMI.

Office for Standards in Education (2004) *Ofsted Subject Reports 2002/03: Physical Education in Secondary Schools*. London. Ofsted.

Penney, D. (1999) On the sidelines? Physical Education teachers and the revision of the National Curriculum for Physical Education in England. Paper presented at the *British Educational Research Association Annual Conference*, University of Sussex, 2–5 September.

Penney, D. and Waring, M. (2000) The absent agenda: pedagogy and Physical Education, *Journal of Sport Pedagogy*, 6(1), 4–37.

Placek, J.H. (1983) Conceptions of success in teaching: busy, happy, and good? In T. Templin and J. Olsen (eds) *Teaching in Physical Education*, Champaign, IL: Human Kinetics Publishers.

Putnam, J.W. (1998) *Cooperative Learning and Strategies for Inclusion: Celebrating Diversity in the Classroom* (2nd edition). Baltimore, MD: Brookes.

Qualifications and Curriculum Authority (QCA) (2007) The Secondary Curriculum Review. Available online at www.qca.org.uk/secondarycurriculumreview/index.htm (accessed 21 June 2007).

Qualifications and Curriculum Authority (QCA) (2000) *Physical Education: A Scheme of Work for Key Stages 1 and 2*. London: QCA.

Rink, J.E. (2005) *Teaching Physical Education for Learning* (5th edition). St. Louis, MI: McGraw-Hill Humanities.

Rovegno, I. (2003) Teachers' knowledge construction. In S. Silverman and C. Ennis (eds) *Student Learning in Physical Education: Allying Research to Enhance Instruction*. Champaign, IL: Human Kinetics.

Sewell, A. (2002) Constructivism and student misconceptions: why every teacher needs to know about them, *Australian Science Teachers' Journal*, 48(4), 24–28.

Shulman, L.S. (1987) Knowledge and teaching: foundations of the new reform, *Harvard Educational Review*, 57(1), 1–22.

Siedentop, D. (1994) *Sport Education: Quality PE Through Positive Sport Experiences*. Champaign, IL: Human Kinetics.

Siedentop, D. (2002) Content knowledge for physical education, *Journal of Teaching in Physical Education*, 21, 386–377.

Spence, J. and Haydn-Davies, D. (2011) *Teacher Perceptions Research Report*, for Key Stage 1 Project (Top Foundation).

Stodden, D.F., Goodway, J.D., Langendorfer, S.J., Robertson, M.A., Rudisill, M.E., Garcia, C. and Garcia, L.E. (2008). A developmental perspective on the role of motor skill competence in physical activity: an emergent relationship, *Quest*, 60(2), 290–306.

Teacher Training Agency (1997) The 'Standards for the Award of Qualified Teacher Status'. London: TTA.

Tinning, R. (2006) Theoretical orientations in physical education teacher education. In D. Kirk, D. Macdonald, and M. O'Sullivan (eds) *The Handbook of Physical Education*. London: Sage Publications.

TLRP (2004) *Personalised Learning: A Commentary by the Teaching and Learning Research Programme*. Cambridge: TLRP.

Tsangaridou, N. (2006) Teachers' beliefs. In D. Kirk, D. Macdonald and M. O'Sullivan, (eds) *The Handbook of Physical Education*. London: Sage.

Veal, W. and MaKinster, J. (1999) Pedagogical content knowledge taxonomies, *Electronic Journal of Science Education*, 3(4). Available online at http://wolfweb.unr.edu/homepage/crowther/ejse/vealmak. html (accessed 14 January 2011).

Ward, G. (2012) Examining primary schools' physical education coordinators' pedagogical content knowledge of games: are we just playing as this?, *Education 3–13*, 41(6), 562–585.

Ward, G. and Griggs, G. (2011) Principles of play: a proposed framework towards a holistic overview of games in primary Physical Education, *Education 3–13*, 39(5) 499–516.

Westcott, S.L., Lowes, L.P. and Richardson, P.K. (1997). Evaluation of postural stability in children: current theories and assessment tools, *Physical Therapy*, 77(6), 629–645.

6

PROVIDING EXPERTISE IN PRIMARY PHYSICAL EDUCATION

Leading, linking and outsourcing

Introduction

A subject leader in any given school has the role essentially to provide leadership and direction for the subject. The reality within primary schools can be somewhat removed from this position and the importance of the role of a subject leader can vary enormously ranging from a role holder with a budget delivering staff training to a member of staff simply in charge of a cupboard. Physical Education subject leaders have for a long time belonged to the latter group but this position and its connectedness to the wider education community has shifted considerably over the last two decades. This chapter outlines this journey beginning in the mid-1990s.

Expertise from the subject leader

At a time when four-year teacher training courses were the norm, qualified teachers were entering the profession with not only considerable practice under their belts but a deep knowledge of one chosen area of the national curriculum. Schools would recruit and fill vacancies based on such needs and where possible ensure a wide base of subject specialisms within a staff room. This enabled different members of staff to take on roles as subject leaders acting as the in-house experts for their school. Much was expected of such highly trained individuals illustrated by the National Standards for Subject Leaders (TTA, 1998).

> A subject leader provides leadership and direction for the subject and ensures that it is managed and organised to meet the aims and objectives of the school and the subject. While the headteacher and governors

carry overall responsibility for school improvement, a subject leader has responsibility for securing high standards of teaching and learning in their subject as well as playing a major role in the development of school policy and practice. Throughout their work, a subject leader ensures that practices improve the quality of education provided, meet the needs and aspirations of all pupils, and raise standards of achievement in the school.

A subject leader plays a key role in supporting, guiding and motivating teachers of the subject, and other adults. Subject leaders evaluate the effectiveness of teaching and learning, the subject curriculum and progress towards targets for pupils and staff, to inform future priorities and targets for the subject. The degree to which a subject leader is involved in monitoring to provide the range of information for evaluation will depend on school policy and be influenced by the size of the school. Although the subject leader will undertake a variety of monitoring activities, headteachers in smaller primary schools may retain a larger proportion of that monitoring which requires direct classroom observation of teaching and learning.

A subject leader identifies needs in their own subject and recognises that these must be considered in relation to the overall needs of the school. It is important that a subject leader has an understanding of how their subject contributes to school priorities and to the overall education and achievement of all pupils.

Further expertise for subject leaders could be gained from the Local Education Authority (LEA) who typically had well developed and highly experienced teams dedicated into different aspects of schooling and to each individual subject. A summary of the expertise that subject leaders should demonstrate was provided and this has been collated into the Box 6.1 ('Outcomes of effective subject leadership') which might serve as a useful starting point for those looking for guidance or those wishing to develop recommendations for such a role.

THOUGHT BOX

Think of those whom you may know as subject leaders (including yourself perhaps). How effective are they in meeting the outcomes shown in the box entitled 'Outcomes of effective subject leadership'?

BOX 6.1 OUTCOMES OF EFFECTIVE SUBJECT LEADERSHIP

Outcomes of effective subject leadership results in:

Pupils who show sustained improvement in their subject knowledge, understanding and skills in relation to prior attainment; understand the key ideas in the subject at a level appropriate to their age and stage of development; show improvement in their literacy, numeracy and information technology skills; know the purpose and sequence of activities; are well prepared for any tests and examinations in the subject; are enthusiastic about the subject and highly motivated to continue with their studies; through their attitudes and behaviour, contribute to the maintenance of a purposeful working environment.

Teachers who work well together as a team; support the aims of the subject and understand how they relate to the school's aims; are involved in the formation of policies and plans and apply them consistently in the classroom; are dedicated to improving standards of teaching and learning; have an enthusiasm for the subject which reinforces the motivation of pupils; have high expectations for pupils and set realistic but challenging targets based on a good knowledge of their pupils and the progression of concepts in the subject; make good use of guidance, training and support to enhance their knowledge and understanding of the subject and to develop expertise in their teaching; take account of relevant research and inspection findings; make effective use of subject-specific resources; select appropriate teaching and learning approaches to meet subject specific learning objectives and the needs of pupils.

Parents who are well informed about their child's achievements in the subject and about targets for further improvement; know the expectations made of their child in learning the subject; know how they can support or assist their child's learning in the subject.

Headteachers and other senior managers who understand the needs of the subject; use information about achievements and development priorities in the subject in order to make well informed decisions and to achieve greater improvements in the whole school's development and its aims.

Other adults in the school and community, including technical and administrative staff, classroom assistants, external agencies and representatives of business and industry, who are informed of subject achievements and priorities; are able, where appropriate, to play an effective role in supporting the teaching and learning of the subject.

Professional knowledge and understanding

Subject leaders should have knowledge and understanding of:

a.   their school's aims, priorities, targets and action plans;
b.   the relationship of the subject to the curriculum as a whole;
c.   any statutory curriculum requirements for the subject and the requirements for assessment, recording and reporting of pupils' attainment and progress;
d.   the characteristics of high quality teaching in the subject and the main strategies for improving and sustaining high standards of teaching, learning and achievement for all pupils;
e.   how evidence from relevant research and inspection evidence and local, national and international standards of achievement in the subject can be used to inform expectations, targets and teaching approaches;
f.   how to use comparative data, together with information about pupils' prior attainment, to establish benchmarks and set targets for improvement;
g.   how to develop pupils' literacy, numeracy and information technology skills through the subject;
h.   how teaching the subject can promote pupils' spiritual, moral, social, cultural, mental and physical development;
i.   management, including employment law, equal opportunities legislation, personnel, external relations, finance and change;
j.   how teaching the subject can help to prepare pupils for the opportunities, responsibilities and experiences of adult life;
k.   the current use and future potential of information and communications technology to aid teaching and learning of the subject, and to assist with subject management;
l.   the role of school governance and how it can contribute to the work of the subject leader;
m.   the implications of information and guidance documents from LEAs, the DfEE, WOED and other national bodies and associations;
n.   the implications of the Code of Practice for Special Educational Needs for teaching and learning in their subject;
o.   health and safety requirements, including where to obtain expert advice.

Skills and attributes

a) Leadership skills

1.   Secure commitment to a clear aim and direction for the subject.
2.   Prioritise, plan and organise.
3.   Work as part of a team.
4.   Deal sensitively with people, recognise individual needs and take account

of these in securing a consistent team approach to raising achievement in the subject.

5. Acknowledge and utilise the experience, expertise and contribution of others.
6. Set standards and provide a role model for pupils and other staff, in the teaching and learning of the subject.
7. Devolve responsibilities and delegate tasks, as appropriate.
8. Seek advice and support when necessary.
9. Command credibility through the discharge of their duties and use their expertise to influence others in relation to their subject.
10. Make informed use of research and inspection findings.
11. Apply good practice to and from other subjects and areas.

b) Decision-making skills

1. Judge when to make decisions, when to consult with others, and when to defer to the headteacher or senior managers.
2. Analyse, understand and interpret relevant information and data.
3. Think creatively and imaginatively to anticipate and solve problems and identify opportunities.

c) Communication skills

1. Communicate effectively, orally and in writing, with the headteacher, other staff, pupils, parents, governors, external agencies and the wider community, including business and industry.
2. Negotiate and consult effectively.
3. Ensure good communication with, and between, staff who teach and support the subject.
4. Chair meetings effectively.

d) Self-management skills

1. Prioritise and manage their own time effectively, particularly in relation to balancing the demands made by teaching, subject management and involvement in school development.
2. Achieve challenging professional goals.
3. Take responsibility for their own professional development.

e) Attributes

1. Personal impact and presence.
2. Adaptability to changing circumstances and new ideas.
3. Energy, vigour and perseverance.
4. Self-confidence.

5. Enthusiasm.
6. Intellectual ability.
7. Reliability and integrity.
8. Commitment.

Strategic direction and development

1. Develop and implement policies and practices for the subject which reflect the school's commitment to high achievement, effective teaching and learning.
2. Create a climate which enables other staff to develop and maintain positive attitudes towards the subject and confidence in teaching it.
3. Establish a clear, shared understanding of the importance and role of the subject in contributing to pupils' spiritual, moral, cultural, mental and physical development, and in preparing pupils for the opportunities, responsibilities and experiences of adult life.
4. Use data effectively to identify pupils who are underachieving in the subject and, where necessary, create and implement effective plans of action to support those pupils.
5. Analyse and interpret relevant national, local and school data, plus research and inspection evidence, to inform policies, practices, expectations, targets and teaching methods.
6. Establish, with the involvement of relevant staff, short, medium and long term plans for the development and resourcing of the subject, which:
   a. contribute to whole-school aims, policies and practices, including those in relation to behaviour, discipline, bullying and racial harassment;
   b. are based on a range of comparative information and evidence, including in relation to the attainment of pupils;
   c. identify realistic and challenging targets for improvement in the subject;
   d. are understood by all those involved in putting the plans into practice;
   e. are clear about action to be taken, timescales and criteria for success.
7. Monitor the progress made in achieving subject plans and targets, evaluate the effects on teaching and learning, and use this analysis to guide further improvement.

Teaching and learning

1. Ensure curriculum coverage, continuity and progression in the subject for all pupils, including those of high ability and those with special educational or linguistic needs.

2. Ensure that teachers are clear about the teaching objectives in lessons, understand the sequence of teaching and learning in the subject, and communicate such information to pupils.
3. Provide guidance on the choice of appropriate teaching and learning methods to meet the needs of the subject and of different pupils.
4. Ensure effective development of pupils' literacy, numeracy and information technology skills through the subject.
5. Establish and implement clear policies and practices for assessing, recording and reporting on pupil achievement, and for using this information to recognise achievement and to assist pupils in setting targets for further improvement.
6. Ensure that information about pupils' achievements in previous classes and schools is used effectively to secure good progress in the subject.
7. Set expectations and targets for staff and pupils in relation to standards of pupil achievement and the quality of teaching; establish clear targets for pupil achievement, and evaluate progress and achievement in the subject by all pupils, including those with special educational and linguistic needs.
8. Evaluate the teaching of the subject in the school, use this analysis to identify effective practice and areas for improvement, and take action to improve further the quality of teaching.
9. Ensure effective development of pupils' individual and collaborative study skills necessary for them to become increasingly independent in their work and to complete tasks independently when out of school.
10. Ensure that teachers of the subject are aware of its contribution to pupils' understanding of the duties, opportunities, responsibilities and rights of citizens.
11. Ensure that teachers of the subject know how to recognise and deal with racial stereotyping.
12. Establish a partnership with parents to involve them in their child's learning of the subject, as well as providing information about curriculum, attainment, progress and targets.
13. Develop effective links with the local community, including business and industry, in order to extend the subject curriculum, enhance teaching and to develop pupils' wider understanding.

Leading and managing staff

1. Help staff to achieve constructive working relationships with pupils.
2. Establish clear expectations and constructive working relationships among staff involved with the subject, including through team working and mutual support; devolving responsibilities and delegating tasks, as appropriate; evaluating practice; and developing an acceptance of accountability.

3.   Sustain their own motivation and, where possible, that of other staff involved in the subject.
4.   Appraise staff as required by the school policy and use the process to develop the personal and professional effectiveness of the appraisee(s).
5.   Audit training needs of subject staff.
6.   Lead professional development of subject staff through example and support, and co-ordinate the provision of high quality professional development by methods such as coaching, drawing on other sources of expertise as necessary, for example, higher education, LEAs, subject associations.
7.   Ensure that trainee and newly qualified teachers are appropriately trained, monitored, supported and assessed in relation to standards for the award of Qualified Teacher Status, the Career Entry Profiles and standards for induction.
8.   Enable teachers to achieve expertise in their subject teaching.
9.   Work with the SENCO and any other staff with special educational needs expertise, to ensure that individual education plans are used to set subject-specific targets and match work well to pupils' needs.
10. Ensure that the headteacher, senior managers and governors are well informed about subject policies, plans and priorities, the success in meeting objectives and targets, and subject-related professional development plans.

Efficient and effective deployment of staff and resources

1.   Establish staff and resource needs for the subject and advise the headteacher and senior managers of likely priorities for expenditure, and allocate available subject resources with maximum efficiency to meet the objectives of the school and subject plans and to achieve value for money.
2.   Deploy, or advise the headteacher on the deployment of staff involved in the subject to ensure the best use of subject, technical and other expertise.
3.   Ensure the effective and efficient management and organisation of learning resources, including information and communications technology.
4.   Maintain existing resources and explore opportunities to develop or incorporate new resources from a wide range of sources inside and outside the school.
5.   Use accommodation to create an effective and stimulating environment for the teaching and learning of the subject.
6.   Ensure that there is a safe working and learning environment in which risks are properly assessed.

(Adapted from TTA, 1998)

A seismic shift from specific to generic qualification

Arguably the most significant shift that occurred to irrevocably change the mechanism for maintaining subject knowledge within schools was the publication of 'Qualifying to Teach' (DfES, 2002), the next in a long line of standards and requirements expected of primary trainees. The significance of this document as opposed to its predecessor Circular 4/98 (DfEE, 1998) was that for the first time, 'Qualifying to Teach' did not require trainees to hold an additional subject specialism beyond their basic primary training. The consequences of this shift were rapid. Many universities shifted their training from three and four year undergraduate courses, to one-year postgraduate courses. With less specialist subject teaching required this meant less staff were also needed. Foundation subjects within the National Curriculum such as Physical Education were typically delivered with a minimum provision and where universities had gaps in staffing any shortfall was covered by seconding staff from nearby schools. At the same time local authorities began streamlining their workforces and advisory teachers became phased out with many becoming self employed, hoping to be bought in as Physical Education consultants. This arrangement was sustained in some areas but this dynamic was destabilised again by consecutive significant government policy announcements within Physical Education and school sport – namely, the Physical Education, School Sport and Club Links (PESSCL) strategy and the Physical Education and Sport Strategy for Young People (PESSYP) strategy.

The PESSCL and PESSYP strategies

The phased implementation of two consecutive national strategies transformed the infrastructure of Physical Education and school sport, including the people who work within it and the way they interrelated. In October 2002, the Physical Education, School Sport and Club Links (PESSCL) strategy invested in excess of £1.5 billion into Physical Education and school sport within the UK. The strategy contained eight different strands (Specialist Sports Colleges, Sport Co-ordinators, Gifted and Talented, Investigating Physical Education and School Sport, Step into Sport, Professional Development, School/Club Links and Swimming) with its overall objective to enhance the take-up of sporting opportunities by 5–16 year-olds a public service agreement (PSA) pledged to engage children in at least two hours high quality Physical Education and sport at school each week (DfES/DCMS, 2003). Five years later the expectation on staff to increase their delivery time was raised still further with the injection of another £¾ billion with the introduction of the Physical Education and Sport Strategy for Young People (PESSYP) which was pledged to create a new '5 hour offer' for all (DCSF, 2008).

As with many New Labour and 'New Right' strategies the need to be accountable and to measure the impact of its implementation was quick to follow

(Ball, 2001). The Specialist Sport College strand was further developed from the PESSCL strategy and led to the creation of the School Sport Partnership Programme (SSPP) which included a series of national evaluations.

School sport partnerships

Every School Sport Partnership (SSP) had within its structure a specialist sports college which was connected to a further four to eight secondary schools and their associated cluster of feeder primary schools. Day-to-day management of the SSP was overseen by the Partnership Development Manager (PDM). Located in each secondary school was then a school sport co-ordinator (SSCo) employed for up to a total of two and half days a week to work in partnership with others within the structure, including primary schools.

Early findings reporting on the effectiveness of the implementation of the SSPP indicated a range of positive impacts on Physical Education and sport in schools, including extending the range and provision of extracurricular activities and increasing the number of young people being physically active (Ofsted 2002, 2003, 2004, 2005; Quick and Goddard, 2004; Houlihan and Wong, 2005; Loughborough Partnership, 2005, 2006). In addition, the more recent evaluations of Physical Education and school sport within the SSP system does indicate historic improvements across inter-school and intra-school sports participation levels up to 2010 (DfE 2010a, 2010b, 2010c).

The impact of the SSP system was however contested with the evidence base for these claims questioned and the absence of a clear rationale highlighted. Specifically, 'policy goals articulated in the PESSCL strategy were based less on evidence and practical considerations than on politics and pure emotion' (Smith and Leech, 2010: 336). Reflective of this was the subtle shift from a focus on high quality Physical Education to basic participation statistics. Qualitative data of what was occurring within partnerships was difficult to obtain, yet when it did occur it was again less than glowing in relation to the statistics presented (Flintoff, 2008; Ward and Griggs, 2010). Further to this, Houlihan and Lindsey (2008) also identified a number of other issues within the SSP system that were worthy of closer scrutiny. These included differential objectives being pursued by clubs and schools and how this affected the opportunities for young people. In some 'partnerships the relationship is less fruitful with the local authority seeing the SSP as a competitor in the out-of-school hours market for young people' (Houlihan and Lindsey, 2008: 231). The SSP programme finally reached a point under the new coalition government at which, due to reduced or removed funding, the network became increasingly fragmented and in most regions largely dismantled (Pitt and Rockwood, 2011).

Despite the disputed benefits of the SSP, qualitative research following the breakup of the network revealed practitioners identified that the break down in partnerships was an obvious loss in cross school collaboration, facilitation of inter-school planning of events and development of communication (Mackintosh, 2012). The piecemeal arrangements that followed from area to area are reflective of other studies examining sport partnership development (Lindsey, 2006; Houlihan and Lindsey, 2008; Mackintosh, 2011). As Mackintosh (2012: 439) identified:

> The loss of eight years of development of relationships across the primary, secondary and community sectors will be hard to replace ... the longer term picture of the real impact of the dismantling of the SSP infrastructure ... remains to be seen. However, what is clear is that primary physical education appears to have been a key loser in this policy transition and that a new tier of problems for practice may have unexpectedly been generated.

Primary link teachers

Within each SSP a primary schools a primary link teacher (PLT) was appointed who could theoretically at least be released from teaching for twelve days per year. In their role, PLTs were to advocate high quality physical education and coordinate and support school sport opportunities. Overall they were tasked with sharing good practice with school colleagues, developing and ensuring implementation of after school sport programmes, using sport to support transition from primary school to secondary, developing programmes to engage non participants and to work with others to support transition in to local clubs (YST, 2008: 9).

Findings by Griggs and Ward (2010) indicated that PLTs were largely passive recipients of targets, surveillance and accountability handed down from their SSCo. The meeting of prescriptive targets became bewildering for some, lacking relevance to the school specific context. The lack of ownership was not aided by how hard many appeared to find the role as it demanded much more than simply twelve days of release from teaching duties, which partnership funding allowed. An added issue was created by the rural geography of the area which necessitated many events and competitions to be held in curriculum time. This placed a further demand on the teacher release funding, compounding the issue of time to complete the jobs the PLT role created.

Of most concern was how PLTs saw their inability to directly affect the raising of standards and delivery of High Quality Physical Education lessons. Key to any raising standards agenda in schools, both internal and external, has been the implementation of a regular policy of monitor and review. Yet despite the twelve funded days a year PLTs were given within their role, not one of the PLTs questioned in the research used the time for such a purpose in either their own school or any other. Most felt unable given their lack of experience or training, typical of the sector (indicated in Chapter 4) and if some expertise could not be gained directly within the SSP many saw sport coaches as the solution.

Outsourcing Physical Education and school sport: the use of sports coaches

With a landscape of limited teacher training, low levels of teacher confidence and inadequate CPD highlighted in Chapter 4, changes in government policy began to impact upon Physical Education provision still further. First, in order to meet such ambitious PSA targets of engaging children in two hours high quality Physical Education and sport at school each week, which was later raised to five hours, the number of adults other than teachers (AOTTs) used in primary schools, such as sports coaches, increased dramatically (Lavin et al., 2008). Second, the implementation of the 'National Agreement for Raising Standards and Tackling Workload' (DfES, 2003) began to remodel and broaden the school workforce in England, 'designed to tackle the problem of workload, and the crisis in teacher recruitment and retention' (Gunter, 2007: 1). Consequently, since 1 September 2005 all teachers have had an entitlement to a guaranteed minimum of 10 per cent of their timetabled teaching commitment for planning, preparation and assessment (PPA). With an apparent underlying willingness of primary schools to give up delivery of curriculum Physical Education (Griggs, 2010) and the need to cover the 10 per cent shortfall in staffing, many schools opted to employ sports coaches to deliver Physical Education lessons for as little as £20 per hour rather than employ further qualified teaching staff (Griggs, 2010).

The opportunity to be involved in primary school physical education and sport was seized upon by an 'emerging community of degree-qualified sports coaches' (Kirk, 2010: 128). At first many delivered extracurricular activities but over time the opportunities to deliver Physical Education lessons in curriculum time increased (Griggs, 2010). Many embraced the employment of often self titled 'multi skilled coaches' as they were able to make a quick impact in meeting targets of raising pupils' levels of participation and engagement in a wider range of activities (Lyle and Dowens, 2013; Ofsted, 2006, 2011). It also enabled primary schools to better manage the constraints associated with several other educational processes (Smith, 2013). These processes have included: rising class sizes; increased emphasis on standards in literacy and numeracy; local management of budgets; and the inclusion of Physical Education in an already crowded and pressured curriculum timetable (Griggs, 2010; Blair and Capel, 2011, 2013; Rainer et al., 2012).

Concerns were raised from the outset (Griggs, 2007, 2008; Blair and Capel, 2008a, 2008b; Lavin et al., 2008) about: the extent to which coaches lack appropriate teaching qualifications, prioritise activities and sporting objectives over educational goals and lack class management skills (Blair and Capel, 2011; Griggs, 2010). Also their employment removes responsibility for the delivery of Physical Education from the class teacher, resulting in them becoming progressively and further deskilled (Keay and Spence, 2012). In summary Blair and Capel (2013: 176) conclude that:

[C]oaches who have learnt to coach through NGB awards and through their own experiences are unlikely to have the background, experience or knowledge, skill and understanding in relation to working within the NCPE. Formal coach education courses do not adequately prepare coaches for working with pupils in the NCPE (in terms of content) or delivering extra-curricular provision ... or indeed for working with young people inside and outside of school in terms of pedagogy and reflective practice.

That said, the practice of teachers and coaches working together has become more prevalent, accepted and normalised (Green, 2008). During this growing relationship, to secure their perceived weakened position in schools, many coaches have committed to a growing professionalisation of sports coaching (Smith, 2013) placing a renewed emphasis on gaining appropriate coaching awards and NGB qualifications (Taylor and Garratt, 2010). This has been encouraged by government policies where those working with and within the public sector will 'gain certification in a culture of performativity and credentialism' (Taylor and Garratt, 2013: 33). Though the outsourcing of Physical Education has remained contentious for some, first facilitated by the additional funding made available as a result of the SSP programme, it is widespread in many other countries around the world (Williams et al., 2011). At a time where 'deregulation of the work of teaching to allow non-teaching staff to undertake classroom activities' (Ball, 2013: 167) is accepted, the outsourcing of Physical Education looks set to remain. Despite the lack of evidence determining whether the use of non teaching staff is having a positive impact within schools (Evans and Davies, 2010), given the recent announcement introducing the Primary Sport Premium it seems likely that the outsourcing of Physical Education may in fact expand still further.

THOUGHT BOX

Should Physical Education and school sport ever be outsourced? What are the justifications for the viewpoint reached and would changing circumstances ever change your answer?

The Primary Sport Premium

Following the dismantling of SSPs and under felt pressures to deliver upon on promises of a post Olympic legacy (DCMS, 2007; Griggs and Ward, 2013), in March 2013, the Coalition government announced an investment of ring-fenced funding totalling £150 million per annum until 2015 (DfE, 2013). The expenditure of monies provided (equating to approximately £9,000 for each primary school) is left to the discretion of individual schools for which they are accountable which will be monitored by Ofsted during inspections. The large sums of money available to external companies are obvious who could seek to profit from the multiples of £9,000 available to secure. Indeed, the House of Commons Education Committee (2013: 49) noted that primary school headteachers were met with 'a rush of commercial providers once the funding was announced. This was seen as a danger, with unknowing headteachers taking on commercial providers who were of questionable quality and limited to coaching rather than teaching PE'.

Concerns have been raised that the encouragement for schools to use The Primary Sport Premium in creative ways may exacerbate already widening social inequalities (Evans and Davies, 2010; Ball, 2012, 2013), where schools find themselves locked increasingly into privatised models of Physical Education provision (Smith, 2013). Over time it has been suggested that some parents will look to seek out appropriate schools which are in effect offering forms of privatised Physical Education and school sport to advantage their offspring. (Evans and Davies, 2010: 773) explain that:

> [G]iven this climate, it is not at all surprising that increasingly parents seek, but only some are able to secure, physical educational opportunities for their children through a mix of state and private institutions. And given that parents seek out such opportunities to maintain social advantages for their children, so too a new generation of specialist childhood PE/sport advisers and services have come into play and thrive on the commercial exploitation of their anxieties.

Conclusion

It could be argued that because of the competing demands within primary schools in the twenty-first century and the impact of initiatives of PESSCL, PESSYP and the Primary Sport Premium, that leadership in Physical education is more important than ever before. However, with a workforce that are more generically skilled and less qualified in a more subject specific sense, Physical Education subject leaders are in a more difficult position than ever. An unwavering focus on children's learning and some clear guidelines, shown in Box 6.1 'Outcomes of effective subject leadership' (page 73), should be able to resist the fads and fashions of government policy, professional associations and external providers selling their wares. Within Physical Education in practice, it is often clarity of thought and having courage of ones convictions that marks out effective subject leaders from those who are in charge of a cupboard!

KEY READINGS

The outsourcing of Physical Education has becoming something of a 'hot topic' within primary Physical Education. A good overview of key issues can be obtained from reading a pair of papers – namely Blair, R. and Capel, S. (2011) Primary physical education, coaches and continuing professional development, *Sport, Education and Society*, 16, 485–505, and Griggs, G. (2010) For sale – primary physical education. £20 per hour or nearest offer, *Education 3–13*, 38(1), 39–46. For those wishing to understand more about subject leadership, two older texts are useful here. For a generic overview of primary school subject leadership find, Bell, D. and Ritchie, R. (1999) *Towards Effective Subject Leadership* (London: McGraw-Hill). For issues pertaining to Physical Education, see Raymond, C. (2005) *Co-ordinating Physical Education Across the Primary School* (London: Routledge).

References

Ball, S. (2001) Labour, learning and the economy – a policy sociology perspective. In M. Fielding (ed.) *Taking Education Seriously: Four Years' Hard Labour*. London: Routledge.

Ball, S. (2012) *Global Education Inc. New Policy Networks and the Neo-liberal Imaginary*. London: Routledge.

Ball, S. (2013) *The Education Debate* (2nd edition). Bristol: Policy Press.

Blair, R. and Capel, S. (2008a) The use of coaches to cover planning, preparation and assessment time – some issues, *Primary Physical Education Matters*, 3(2), ix – x.

Blair, R. and Capel, S. (2008b) The use of coaches to cover planning, preparation and assessment time – some issues, *Primary Physical Education Matters*, 3(3), v–vii.

Blair, R. and Capel, S. (2011) Primary physical education, coaches and continuing professional development, *Sport, Education and Society*, 16(4), 485–505.

Blair, R. and Capel, S. (2013) Who should teach physical education in curriculum and extra-curricular time? In S. Capel and M. Whitehead (eds) *Debates in Physical Education*. London: Routledge.

Department for Culture Media and Sport (DCMS) (2007) *Our promise for 2012. How the UK will benefit from the Olympic Games and Paralympic Games*. London: DCMS.

Department for Children, Schools and Families (DCSF) (2008) *Physical Education and Sport Strategy for Young People*. London: DCSF.

Department for Education (DfE) (2010a) Letter from Michael Gove to Baroness Sue Campbell, Youth Sport Trust, 20 October 2010. London: DfE.

Department for Education (DfE) (2010b) A new approach for school sports: decentralising power, incentivising competition, trusting teachers. Press notice, 20 December 2010. London.

Department for Education (DfE) (2010c) *PE and Sport Survey 2009/10*. London: DfE/TNSBMRB.

Department for Education (DFf) (2013) Primary school PE and sport funding. Available online at www.education.gov.uk/schools/adminandfinance/financialmanagement/b00222858/primary-schoolsport-funding/Primar (accessed 5 March 2014).

Department for Education and Employment (DfEE) (1998) *Physical and Mental Fitness to Teach of Teachers and of Entrants to Initial Teacher Training*. London: DfEE.

DfES (2002) *Qualifying to Teach' Professional Standards for Qualified Teacher Status and Requirements for Initial Teacher Training*. London: DfES

Department for Education and Skills (DfES) (2003) *Raising Standards and Tackling Workload: A National Agreement*. London: DfES.

Department for Education and Skills/Department for Culture, Media and Sport (DfES/DCMS) (2003) *Learning Through Physical Education and Sport: A Guide to the Physical Education, School Sport and Club Links Strategy*. London: DfES/DCMS.

Evans, J. and Davies, B. (2010) Family, class and embodiment: why school physical education makes so little difference to post-school participation patterns in physical activity, *International Journal of Qualitative Studies in Education*, 23, 765–784.

Flintoff, A. (2008) Targeting Mr Average: participation, gender equity and school sport partnerships, *Sport, Education and Society*, 13(4), 393–411.

Green, K. (2008) *Understanding Physical Education*. London: Sage.

Griggs, G. (2007) Outsiders inside: the use of sports coaches in primary schools in the West Midlands. Poster presentation at the annual conference for the British Educational Research Association. 5–8 September, University of London.

Griggs, G. (2008) Outsiders inside: the use of sports coaches in primary schools in the West Midlands, *Physical Education Matters*, 3(2), 33–36.

Griggs, G. (2010) For sale – primary Physical Education. £20 per hour or nearest offer, *Education 3–13*, 38(1), 39–46.

Griggs, G. and Ward, G. (2010) 'Cogs in the machine': unheard voices of primary link teachers, *Primary Physical Education Matters*, 5(1), 3–6.

Griggs, G. and Ward, G. (2013) The London 2012 legacy for primary physical education: policy by the way? Sociological Research Online. Available online at http://www.socresonline.org.uk/18/3/13.html (accessed 22 January 2015).

Gunter, H. (2007) Remodelling the school workforce in England: a study in tyranny, *Journal for Critical Education Policy Studies*, 5(1). Available online at www.jceps.com/index.php?pageID=article&articleID=84 (accessed 12 February 2009).

Houlihan, B. and Lindsey, I. (2008) Networks and partnerships in sports development. In V. Girginov (ed.) *Management of Sports Development*. Oxford: Elsevier.

Houlihan, B. and Wong, C. (2005) *Report on the 2004 National Survey of Specialist Sports Colleges*. Loughborough, Institute of Youth Sport: Loughborough University.

House of Commons Education Committee (2013) *School Sport Following London 2012: No More Political Football*. London: TSO.

Keay, J. and Spence, J. (2012) Addressing training and development needs in primary physical education. In G. Griggs (ed.) *An Introduction to Primary Physical Education*. London: Routledge.

Kirk, D. (2010) *Physical Education Futures*. London: Routledge.

Lavin, J., Swindlehurst, G. and Foster, V. (2008) The use of coaches, adults supporting learning and teaching assistants in the teaching of physical education in the primary school, *Primary Physical Education Matters*, 3(1), ix–xi.

Lindsey, I. (2006) Local partnerships in the United Kingdom for the new opportunities for PE and sport programme: a network analysis, *European Sport Management Quarterly*, 6(2), 167–85.

Loughborough Partnership (2005) *School Sport Partnerships: Annual Monitoring and Evaluation Report for 2004*. Loughborough, Institute of Youth Sport: Loughborough University.

Loughborough Partnership (2006) *School Sport Partnerships: Annual Monitoring and Evaluation Report for 2005*. Loughborough, Institute of Youth Sport: Loughborough University.

Lyle, J. and Dowens, T. (2013) Sport development and sport coaching. In K. Hylton (ed.) *Sport Development: Policy, Process and Practice* (3rd edition). London: Routledge.

Mackintosh, C. (2011) An analysis of county sport partnerships in England: the fragility, challenges and complexity of partnership working in sports development, *International Journal of Sport Policy and Politics*, 3(1): 45–64.

Mackintosh, C. (2012) Dismantling the school sport partnership infrastructure: findings from a survey of physical education and school sport practitioners, *Education 3-13*, 42(4): 432–449:

Office for Standards in Education (2002) *The School Sport Co-ordinator Programme: Evaluation of Phases 1 and 2, 2001–2003*. London: HMSO.

Office for Standards in Education (2003) *The School Sport Co-ordinator Programme: Evaluation of Phases 1 and 2, 2001–2003*. London: HMSO.

Office for Standards in Education (2004) *The School Sport Partnership Programme: Evaluation of Phases 3 and 4, 2003*. London: HMSO.

Office for Standards in Education (2005) *Physical Education in Primary Schools*. London: TSO.

Office for Standards in Education (2006) *School Sport Partnerships: A Survey of Good Practice*. London: HMSO.

Office for Standards in Education (2011) *School Sport Partnerships: A Survey of Good Practice*. London: HMSO.

Pitt, E. and Rockwood, J. (2011) Waving a white flag? Examining developments in school sport ideology and the implications for coaching and educational provision. Paper presented at the political studies association – Sport under pressure conference, 18 March 2011, in University of Birmingham.

Quick, S. and Goddard, S. (2004) *Schools in the School Sport Partnership Programme: PE, School Sports and Club Links Survey 2003–4*. London: Department for Education and Skills.

Rainer, P., Cropley, B., Jarvis, S. and Griffiths, R. (2012) From policy to practice: the challenges of providing high quality physical education and school sport faced by head teachers within primary schools, *Physical Education and Sport Pedagogy*, 17, 429–446.

Smith, A. (2013) Primary school physical education and sports coaches: evidence from a study of school sport partnerships in north-west England, *Sport, Education and Society*, doi: 10.1080/13573322.2013.847412.

Smith, A. and Leech, R. (2010) 'Evidence. What evidence?': Evidence-based policy making and school sport partnerships in north-west England, *International Journal of Sport Policy*, 2(3), 327–345.

Taylor, W. and Garratt, D. (2010) The professionalisation of sports coaching: relations of power, resistance and compliance, *Sport, Education and Society*, 15(1), 121–139.

Taylor, W. and Garratt, D. (2013) Coaching and professionalisation. In P. Potrac, W. Gilbert, and J. Denison (eds) *The Routledge Handbook of Sports Coaching*. London: Routledge.

Teacher Training Agency (TTA) (1998) *National Standards for Subject Leaders*. London: TTA.

Ward, G. (2012) Examining primary schools' physical education coordinators' pedagogical content knowledge of games: are we just playing as this?, *Education 3–13*, iFirst.

Ward, G. and Griggs, G. (2010) Cogs in the machine – primary link teachers, *Primary Physical Education Matters*, 5(1), 3–4.

Williams, B., Hay, P. and Macdonald, D. (2011) The outsourcing of health, sport and physical educational work: a state of play, *Physical Education and Sport Pedagogy*, 16, 399–415.

Youth Sport Trust (YST) (2008) *The School Element of the 5 Hour Offer Guidance Notes on Delivery Roles and Responsibilities*. Loughborough: Youth Sport Trust.

7

DEVELOPING CREATIVITY WITHIN PRIMARY PHYSICAL EDUCATION

Introduction

Creativity has become a buzzword in contemporary education and is in increasing demand across many spheres (Bailin, 1994). Historically it has been a multifaceted term and continues to have a wide variety of definitions in different disciplines, though in education its usage is often generic and evermore widespread (Maisuria, 2005). Indeed the Open Creativity Centre (OCC) (2003: 2) indicates that 'creativity is seen as a defining characteristic of UK culture in the twenty first century' which has manifested itself in a plethora of government documentation over the last decade (Craft, 2006), most notably for primary schools in 'Creativity and cultural education: all our futures' (NACCCE, 1999), 'National curriculum in England and Wales' (DfEE/QCA, 1999a), 'Curriculum guidance for the foundation stage' (QCA/DfES, 2000) and 'Excellence and enjoyment: a strategy for primary schools' (DfES, 2003a).

Yet despite such an overt commitment to the development of creativity, the realities within primary schools appear somewhat different, with teachers delivering a narrow focus within any given programme of study (Compton, 2007) as 'most headteachers and subject leaders have concentrated on the raising standards agenda' (OFSTED, 2005a: 2) leading to creativity being underdeveloped in primary schools (OFSTED, 2004). With a heightened awareness of a results and an outcomes-driven system, it is perhaps not surprising that measurable performance has been given greater value (Ball, 2003) to the point where 'performativity' can be seen to be 'hijacking the creativity discourse' (Turner-Bisset, 2007: 201).

Nowhere has this impact been more sharply felt than in foundation subjects such as Physical Education, which have become increasingly marginalised within curriculum time, as a greater emphasis has been placed upon the teaching of core subjects such as English (Literacy), Mathematics (Numeracy) and Science for which annual results are published for all primary schools (see Chapters 2 and 3 for a fuller explanation). In addition, an uneven and an imbalanced physical education curriculum (often dominated by games) delivered in many schools (OFSTED, 1999; Capel, 2000), often by poorly prepared teachers (see Chapter 4), does little to develop the subject or develop pupils' 'higher order' thinking associated with concepts such as creativity.

Though Chedzoy (2006: 4) argues that Physical Education continues to have many avenues to foster creativity, often because it allows pupils the opportunity to make up their own games or their own sequences in gymnastics or dance, this aspect alone is insufficient. In a learning environment not conducive to creativity, such a task could easily be reduced to pupils reproducing 'safe', 'taught' choices so 'not to get it wrong' (Davis, 2000) or simply floundering because they do not have the knowledge and understanding or confidence to cope. The environment created by schools and by the teachers within them is therefore key (Wyse and Spendlove, 2007) and while it is not expected that practitioners should feel an obligation to develop anything approaching 'sublime' creativity (Cropley, 2001), they can do much to encourage what Craft (2000) describes as 'small c' creativity.

THOUGHT BOX

How would you encourage creativity in practice? Can it be done in all areas of Physical Education?

Among the most useful of suggested models to be found for the practical application of developing creativity in schools is that of Nickerson (1999: 409), who identified the following seven key points.

1   Support domain-specific knowledge: pupils need to understand as much as possible about the domain (often subject area) in which they are doing the creative work.
2   Reward curiosity and exploration.
3   Build motivation, particularly internal motivation.
4   Encourage risk taking.
5   Have high expectations/beliefs about creative potential of students: this applies to both teachers' views and students' self-image.
6   Give opportunities for choice and discovery.
7   Develop students self-management skills.

The purpose of this chapter therefore is to explore each of Nickerson's key points listed above, in order to examine key issues and construct some 'real' recommendations for how this could manifest itself within primary Physical Education.

Support domain-specific knowledge

In order for children to realise their creative potential in the physical domain it is imperative that they are equipped with the basic skills with which to be creative. However, this is considerably more problematic than it may first appear. Literature over the last decade, including Evans et al. (1996), Gilbert (1998), Harrison (1998), Oxley (1998), Davies (1999), Revell (2000), Speednet (2000), Warburton (2001) and Wright (2004), has served to highlight that the national curriculum for Physical Education (NCPE) in England and Wales (DfEE/QCA, 1999b) is being delivered ineffectively in primary schools. The root of the problem has been identified repeatedly as the lack of preparedness of wave after wave of primary and junior school teachers to teach physical education (Williams, 1985; Morgan, 1997; Caldecott et al., 2006), with a lack of time given to the subject during teacher training (PEA, 1984; Williams, 1985; Carney and Armstrong, 1996; Morgan, 1997; Clay, 1999; Warburton, 2001), which has reduced significantly as a greater focus has been placed upon the training of core subjects (OFSTED, 1998).

As a direct result of such concerns, much of the literature within primary Physical Education has focused upon both conceptual and practical ways to improve children's key developmental movements (see Pickup et al., 2007 for a summary). 'Physical Literacy' (Whitehead, 2001), 'Basic Moves' (Jess and Dewar, 2004) and 'Fundamental Movement Skills' (STEPS PD, 2007) all seek to wrap the essence of what children need to learn in the physical domain in order to have 'the basic building blocks' (Haydn-Davies, 2005: 48) and a secure foundation for lifelong physical activity. What is imperative is that whichever approach emerges as the 'chosen' vehicle for primary Physical Education, practitioners embrace it wholeheartedly and feel secure, empowered and self-confident in themselves to deliver the programme to their pupils. OFSTED (2005b: 3) identified 'weak subject knowledge' as the major limitation to developing the more challenging and creative aspects of learning.

One possible way forward would be to build on the foundations already laid down in the early years. Examples have been in schemes such as Surestart (DfES, 2003b), a framework that aimed to support a child from birth to three years of age, placing a strong emphasis on a young child's health and physical well being as well as fostering their creative processes. The Foundation Stage, introduced as a distinct phase of education for children aged from three to five years, had both 'physical development' and 'creative development' as two of its seven Early Learning Goals (QCA/DfES, 2000). What is clear from such structures is that both the physicality and the creativity of the child are valued here, evident in their embedment. This was not matched in the national curriculum thinking where discrete subjects such as Physical Education and creativity remained little more than an interesting sideshow. This situation of the last decade is perhaps best summed up by Compton (2007: 115) commenting that 'it is ironic that the youngest children are given the greatest responsibility for their own learning but tragic that this is gradually eroded as the children journey through school'.

Reward curiosity and exploration

Among the repeated references made to creativity in government documentation already outlined, there can be found a recurring theme of focusing upon objectives and outcomes (Turner-Bisset, 2007). No clearer example can be found than on the former QCA website which was set up to promote and guide creativity in the classroom. One exemplar of good practice was entitled: 'A teacher talks about going with the flow while maintaining the focus on learning objectives' (QCA, 2007a: 4). Such statements appear somewhat paradoxical when to many, creativity represents 'open mindedness, exploration, the celebration of difference and … is taken to be an automatic opposition to the language of targets, to instrumental skills, the measurement of outcomes and the dogmas of accountability' (Cullingford, 2007: 133).

This state of affairs serves as a barometer of the current climate where politicians and the media alike associate notions of creativity as progressive, woolly and equated with a fall in standards (Marshall, 2001). Indeed, Maisuria (2005: 145) warns that 'a teacher who is creative and celebrates creativity from pupils is a teacher who is willing to risk a great deal'. Physical Education is not immune to such pressures and in many respects falls victim to an outcome-driven curriculum not just through its educational association but through its association with sport. There is arguably little room for creativity for those teaching discrete skills such as swimming strokes within Physical Education to give but one example. Though those within sport may wax lyrical about moments of creativity performed by its heroes, where a player is beaten or a shot or a delivery is brilliant because of its unorthodoxy, its 'coaching' preaches a discourse of performance and practice and continues to impose this upon physical education curricula (Capel, 2000). Indeed, with the increasing trend of utilising sports coaches in primary school to deliver Physical Education lessons (see Chapter 6) there is a danger that Physical Education experiences may be reduced to repetitive game related skill practices (drills) learned on National Governing Body (NGB) coaching courses.

In a bid to offset the irresistible drift towards a product and outcomes focused Physical Education curriculum, it is essential that the process of learning is also given value. If, during the teaching of gymnastics, only polished sequences of prescribed movements are celebrated, then there is little incentive for a child to explore what other movements their body is capable of. That is not to say that a movement such as a 'textbook' forward roll is not a desirable skill to acquire but ideally this would have been selected by the child as one of a dozen different rolls at their disposal, after repeated exploration. In addition, some such lessons may not always have an observable outcome (Pullman, 2003; Turner-Bisset, 2007). Within the classroom Claxton (2006) advocates the celebration of the creative process by keeping and showing 'drafts' together with 'best' work. In a practical sense this is less obvious though an equivalent may be to record and showcase the different movements tried, along with an explanation of the choices made which were involved in the creation of the final sequence.

Build motivation, particularly internal motivation

Research undertaken by Jeffrey (2006) served to highlight characteristics that were common to creativity practice across a wide variety of teaching and learning environments. The project entitled 'Creative Learning and Student Perspectives' (CLASP) identified four common themes: innovation, ownership, control and relevance. What became apparent within these four themes was how creativity developed as pupils saw their learning as meaningful, took greater ownership and felt in control. What results as pupils internalised the process is that they appeared 'self-motivated, not governed by extrinsic factors, or purely task-oriented exercises' (Jeffrey, 2006: 401).

Physical Education is in an ideal position to capture and capitalise upon what appears to be a child's desire to move (Bailey et al., 2007) but rather than to continue to inculcate a legacy of failure and dropping out of physical activity, so prevalent among adolescents (Sport England, 2003), a new direction must be sought which has greater relevance to children's worlds and interests so they are more equipped to engage in a range of activities throughout their lives. If this can be addressed through imaginative curriculum design and delivery, then Woods (2002: 7) suggests that the likelihood of developing creative individuals is enhanced, explaining that 'relevance aids identification, motivation, excitement and enthusiasm. Control, in turn, leads to ownership of the knowledge that results. If relevance, control and ownership apply, the greater the chance of creative learning resulting.'

Encourage risk taking

Although the publication of 'Excellence and enjoyment: a strategy for primary schools' (DfES, 2003a: 33) sought to invigorate the wider curriculum with its repeated references to creativity and making 'learning vivid and real', Alexander (2004: 14) indicated that these intentions were more 'contradictory than at first sight they seem'. Closer attention to detail reveals that a truer aim was to spread the pedagogy of the literacy and numeracy strategies across the curriculum (Turner-Bissett, 2007) 'identifying the key teaching and learning approaches that the strategies have promoted and transfer them more widely' (DfES, 2003a: 1). Ball (2003) suggests that as a consequence of valuing the fast-paced and interactive approaches advocated by such strategies, this has indeed become the dominant pedagogy within the primary curriculum to the detriment of all others, stifling creativity (Davis, 2000; Turner-Bissett, 2007) and encouraging teachers to avoid taking risks and to 'stay within the box, and keep the pupils there too' (Maisuria, 2005: 143).

In many ways this has physically occurred within Physical Education as schools have leaned towards the delivery of a narrow and imbalanced curriculum (OFSTED, 1999; Capel, 2000), focusing on more indoor activities of gymnastics and dance and a foray outside for some games. Far less attention (and in some cases little or none) is given to Swimming (TES/CCPR, 2003), Athletics or Outdoor and Adventurous Activities (OAA) (OFSTED, 1999; 2005b; Warburton, 2001). In the case of the latter, risks have sought to be eliminated all together as teaching unions have recommended that children should not be taken outside the school perimeter due to the compensation culture and fear of litigation faced by staff should an accident occur (Clare, 2004).

The realities are of course that risks are everywhere, both perceived and real, and what is needed is a sense of perspective and a good dose of risk awareness and risk management. This is as applicable to unions as it is to school, teachers and even children. If children are educated in an environment that is risk averse this severely restricts their creative potential, so modelling an approach that is prepared to consider the broadest range of options is so very important (Craft, 2005).

Have high expectations

Though OFSTED (2005b; 2009) reports that the quality of teaching and of pupil achievement in physical education has improved steadily, compared to core subjects which are externally tested and monitored, there continue to be low expectations of and within Physical Education which have remained unchanged for some time. According to Casbon (2006: 15), 'a few schools are beginning to explore how they can realistically expect higher levels of achievement from a greater proportion of pupils, but this culture is proving slow to change'. In a bid to give guidance as to what high expectations might look like, documents entitled 'High quality in Physical Education and school sport' (DfES, 2004) and 'Do you have high quality Physical Education and sport in your school?' (DfES, 2005) were published, though the impact of these remained unclear.

What is clear however is the link between weak subject knowledge discussed previously and low expectations and the ability of teachers to transmit their own insecurities. 'If for instance we teach in a less than enthusiastic manner, with closed body language and fail to change into appropriate clothing (just putting trainers on instead of shoes is not enough), then this sends a clear message of what our expectations are of this lesson' (Griggs, 2007b: 3). If practitioners are capable of both encouragement and modelling of good practice in the physical domain, then they will move children beyond mere participation or simply being 'busy, happy, and good' (Placek, 1983) and open up the possibilities of higher learning.

Give opportunities for choice and discovery

Physical Education literature continues to celebrate its ability to offer opportunities to make choices and engage in episodes of discovery (Chedzoy, 2006; QCA, 2007b). Upon examination of examples given in guidance for practitioners many opportunities point towards examples of 'guided discovery' which is designed to lead pupils to a planned, predetermined response (Katone, 1949). 'This structure gets the learner to the target with maximum efficiency' (Mosston and Ashworth, 2002: 220) and is consistent with performativity discourses which specify both objectives and outcomes and is the basis for much of the structure found in QCA planning (QCA, 2000), prevalent in planning for primary school physical education. As a method of discovery however this approach has its limits, not least because cognitively it is allied to memory recall and practice (Bruner, 1961). Indeed recent research in primary education by both Alexander (2004) and Moyles et al. (2003) found that dominant pedagogical strategies have reduced teacher–pupil interaction to be 'dominated by closed questions, brief answers which teachers do not build upon, phatic praise rather than diagnostic feedback, and an emphasis on recalling information rather than on speculating and problem solving' (Alexander, 2004: 21).

Physical education must clearly have great creative potential as there is an endless range of movement possibilities that can be combined and recombined but unlocking this potential requires the right tool. One possible solution is to employ a divergent discovery approach where the learner makes most of the key decisions and is engaged cognitively throughout in a process of designing and evaluation (Mosston and Ashworth, 2002). To employ this approach successfully a less constrained learning environment and the use of precise language are key. For example, gymnastic sequencing must go beyond the practice pedagogy and vocabulary of 'Show or find three ways to ...' to a more open 'Create five different movements from a stimulus and connect using ...' where the teacher merely specifies guiding parameters.

Develop students self-management skills

With risk averse practitioners who have weak subject knowledge, as already discussed, it is no surprise that OFSTED (2005b: 3) should report that within primary physical education 'many lack confidence in allowing pupils the freedom to explore'. As a result lessons can quickly fall into the habit of being command style affairs where teachers seek to maximise control, talk a lot and pupils follow their instructions (Mosston and Ashworth, 2002) (see Chapter 5). Though Chedzoy (2006: 4) argues that Physical Education continues to have many avenues to foster creativity through self-management, as it allows opportunity to make up games or sequences, this aspect must be handled carefully. For example, in a learning environment in which only performance and high quality outcomes are celebrated pupils will readily produce 'safe', 'taught' choices so as 'not to get it wrong' (Davis, 2000).

The creation of an inclusive learning environment where children are truly empowered to make their own choices is paramount (Jeffrey and Craft, 2004). Such an ethos takes a real commitment and the patience and confidence to let children manage their own time, resources and wider learning rather than feel the need to prescribe it all for them because of what has been planned for this week and next on a scheme of work.

THOUGHT BOX

Which of Nickerson's seven points would be easiest to implement and which would be more difficult? Are there any further points that might be added for Physical Education?

Conclusion

With creativity having such prominence in twenty first century primary education, it is imperative that Physical Education maximises its potential as an ideal vehicle for exploration and self-expression. Though the effectiveness and implementation of 'Excellence and enjoyment: a strategy for primary schools' (DfES, 2003a) is hotly contested as a means by which to foster creativity, research on the issue has shown schools seeking greater thematic connectivity between subjects (Ward and Bloom, 2007). However, such evidence also reveals the disconnectedness of Physical Education within the primary curriculum as 'only 6% taught Physical Education this way' (Ward, 2007: 14).

As Craft (2005) indicates, it is problematic for practitioners to grasp what is really meant by creativity in practice, so models such as Nickerson's (1999), which sets out to support domain specific knowledge, reward curiosity and exploration, build motivation, encourage risk taking, have high expectations, give opportunities for choice and discovery and develop students self-management skills can serve as a useful structure from which to work.

However, in a climate where the dominant discourse in practice remains that of 'performativity', its effectiveness is still at the mercy of the practitioners who actually develop the planning, deliver the lessons and create the learning environment. Turner-Bisset (2007: 201) warns that presently current pedagogy has a tendency to reduce such models to a checklist mentality, where 'the concern becomes not "what do I want my pupils to learn, and how best will they learn it?" but "have I got creativity covered in my planning?"' This also remains a very real concern too for the future implementation in practice of either 'Physical Literacy' (Whitehead, 2001), 'Basic Moves' (Jess and Dewar, 2004) or 'Fundamental Movement Skills' (STEPS PD, 2007).

If creativity is to truly manifest itself and have value within Physical Education, then far greater risks have to be taken at all levels within education 'in an atmosphere in which the teacher's creative abilities are properly engaged' (NACCCE, 1999: 90). This would model to children the very values so fervently espoused by guiding documentation and would provide a very real opportunity for both 'excellence and enjoyment' to actually occur.

KEY READINGS

In recent years two books in particular have fully embraced the spirit of creativity in Physical Education and successfully managed to link theory to practice. These are: Lavin, J. (ed.) (2008) *Creative Approaches to Physical Education: Helping Children to Achieve Their True Potential* (London: Routledge) and Pickard, A. and Maude, P. (2014) *Teaching Physical Education Creatively* (London: Routledge).

References

Alexander, R. (2004) Still no pedagogy? Principle, pragmatism and compliance in primary education, *Cambridge Journal of Education*, 34(1), 7–33.

Association for Physical Education (afPE) (n.d.) Supporting the delivery of physical education and school sport. Available online at www.afpe.org.uk/ (accessed 24 June 2007).

Bailey, R., Doherty, J. and Pickup, I. (2007) Physical Development and Physical Education. In J. Riley (ed.) *Learning in the Early Years: A Guide for Teachers of Children 3–7* (2nd edition). London: Paul Chapman Publishing.

Bailin, S. (1994) *Achieving Extraordinary Ends*. Norwood, NJ: Ablex Publishing.

Ball, S.J. (2003) The teacher's soul and the terrors of performativity, *Journal of Education Policy*, 18(2), 215–228.

Bruner, J.S. (1961) The act of discovery, *Harvard Educational Review*, 31, 21–32.

Caldecott, S., Warburton, P. and Waring, M. (2006) A survey of the time devoted to the preparation of primary and junior school trainee teachers to teach Physical Education in England, *Physical Education Matters*, 1(1), 45–48.

Capel, S. (2000) Re-reflecting on priorities for physical education: now and in the twenty first century. In S. Capel and S. Piotrowski (eds) *Issues in Physical Education*. London: Routledge.

Carney, C. and Armstrong, N. (1996) The provision of physical education in primary initial teacher training courses in England and Wales, *European Physical Education Review*, 2(1), 64–74.

Casbon, C. (2006) The secret behind achievement, *Physical Education Matters*, 1(1), 15–17.

Chedzoy, S. (2006) Children, creativity and Physical Education. Primary physical education matters, *Physical Education Matters*, 1(1), 4–5.

Clare, J. (2004) Union tells teachers to end all school trips, *Daily Telegraph*, 19 February.

Claxton, G. (2006) Thinking at the edge: developing soft creativity, *Cambridge Journal of Education*, 36(3), September 2006, 351–362.

Clay, G. (1999) Movement backwards and forwards; the influence of government on physical education – an HMI perspective, *British Journal of Physical Education*, 30(4), 38–41.

Compton, A. (2007) Bringing creativity back into primary education, *Education 3–13*, 35(2),109–116.

Craft, A. (2000) *Creativity Across the Primary Curriculum: Framing and Developing Practice.* London: Routledge Falmer.

Craft, A. (2005) *Creativity in Schools: Tensions and Dilemmas.* London: Routledge.

Craft, A. (2006) Fostering creativity with wisdom, *Cambridge Journal of Education*, 36(3), September 2006, 337–350.

Cropley, A. (2001) *Creativity in Education and Learning.* London: Kogan Page.

Cullingford, C. (2007) Creativity and pupils' experience of school, *Education 3–13*, 35(2) 133–142.

Davies, H.J. (1999) Standards in physical education in England at Key Stage 1 and Key Stage 2, past, present and future, *European Review of Physical Education*, 4(2), 173–188.

Davis, T. (2000) Confidence! Its role in the creative teaching and learning of design and technology, *Journal of Technology Education*, 12(1), 18–31.

Department for Education and Employment/Qualifications and Curriculum Authority (DfEE/QCA) (1999a) *The national curriculum in England and Wales.* London: HMSO.

Department for Education and Employment/Qualifications and Curriculum Authority (DfEE/QCA) (1999b) *The national curriculum in England and Wales: Physical Education.* London: HMSO.

Department for Education and Skills (DfES) (2003a) *Excellence and enjoyment: a strategy for primary schools.* London: DfES.

Department for Education and Skills (DfES) (2003b) *Sure Start: birth to three matters.* London: DfES.

Department for Education and Skills (DfES) (2004) *High Quality in Physical Education and School Sport.* London: DfES.

Department for Education and Skills (DfES) (2005) *Do you have high quality Physical Education and sport in your school?* London: DfES.

Evans, J., Penney, D. and Davies, B. (1996) Back to the future, policy and physical education. In N. Armstrong (ed.) *New Directions in Physical Education: Change and Innovation.* London: Cassell.

Gilbert, R. (1998) Physical Education; the key partner, *British Journal of Physical Education*, 29(1), 18–22.

Griggs, G. (2007a) Physical Education: primary matters, secondary importance, *Education 3–13*, 35(1), 59–69.

Griggs, G. (2007b) *Physical Education: The Essential Toolkit for Primary School Teachers.* Blackburn: Educational Print Services Ltd.

Harrison, P. (1998) Why physical education teachers should reject the new proposals for primary education, *British Journal of Physical Education*, 29(1), 4–6.

Haydn-Davies, D. (2005) How does the concept of physical literacy relate to what is and what could be the practice of Physical Education, *British Journal of Teaching Physical Education*, 36(3), 45–48.

Jeffrey, B. (2006) Creative teaching and learning: towards a common discourse and Practice, *Cambridge Journal of Education*, 36(3), September 2006, 399–414.

Jeffrey, B. and Craft, A. (2004) Teaching creatively and teaching for creativity: distinctions and relationships, *Educational Studies*, 30, 77–87.

Jess, M. and Dewar, K. (2004) Basic moves; developing a foundation for lifelong physical activity, *British Journal of Teaching Physical Education*, 35(2), 23–27.

Katone, G. (1949) *Organising and Memorising.* New York: Columbia University Press.

Maisuria, A. (2005) The turbulent times of creativity in the national curriculum, *Policy Futures in Education*, 3(2), 141–152.

Marshall, B. (2001) Creating danger: the place of the arts in education policy. In A. Craft, B. Jeffrey, M. Leibling (eds) *Creativity in Education*. London: Continuum.

Morgan, I. (1997) The preparation of physical education teachers during initial teacher training, *British Journal of Physical Education*, 28, 18–20.

Mosston, M. and Ashworth, S. (2002) *Teaching Physical Education* (5th edition). London: Pearson Education.

Moyles, J., Hargreaves, L., Merry, R., Paterson, F. and Esart-Sarries, V. (2003) *Interactive Teaching in the Primary School: Digging Deeper into Meanings*. Maidenhead: Open University Press.

National Advisory Committee on Creative and Cultural Education (NACCCE) (1999) *Creativity and cultural education: all our futures – a summary*. London: National Campaign for the Arts.

Nickerson, R. (1999) Enhancing creativity. In R.J. Sternberg (ed.) *Handbook of Creativity*. Cambridge: Cambridge University Press.

OFSTED (1998) *Teaching Physical Education in the Primary School: The Initial Training of Teachers*. London: HMSO.

OFSTED (1999) *Primary Education: A Review of Primary Schools in England, 1994–98*. London: TSO.

OFSTED (2004) *The Annual Report of Her Majesty's Chief Inspector of Schools 2003/4*. London: TSO.

OFSTED (2005a) *Primary National Strategy: An Evaluation of its Impact in Primary Schools 2004/5*. London: TSO.

OFSTED (2005b) *Physical Education in Primary Schools*. London: TSO.

OFSTED (2009) *Physical Education in schools: 2005/2008 working towards 2012 and beyond*. London: TSO.

Open Creativity Centre (2003) About us: rationale. Available online at www.opencreativty. ac.uk (accessed 1 June 2007).

Oxley, J. (1998) Never mind literacy and numeracy what about physical education?, *Bulletin of Physical Education*, 29(1), 55–57.

PEA (1984) *Report of a Committee Enquiry, Physical Education in Schools*. London, PEA.

Pickup, I., Haydn-Davies, D., and Jess, M. (2007) The importance of primary physical education, *Physical Education Matters*, 2(1), 8–11.

Placek, J.H. (1983). Conceptions of success in teaching: busy, happy, and good? In T. Templin and J. Olsen (eds) *Teaching in Physical Education*. Champaign, IL: Human Kinetics Publishers.

Pullman, P. (2003) Lost the plot, *The Guardian*, 30 September.

Qualifications and Curriculum Authority (QCA) (2000) *Physical Education: a Scheme of Work for Key Stages 1 and 2*. London: QCA.

Qualifications and Curriculum Authority/Department for Education and Skills QCA/ DfES (2000) *Curriculum guidance for the foundation stage*. London: QCA.

QCA (2007a) Creativity: find it, promote it. Available online at www.ncaction.org.uk/ creativity/promote.htm (accessed 1 June 2007).

QCA (2007b) The Secondary Curriculum Review. Available online at www.qca.org.uk/ secondarycurriculumreview/index.htm (accessed 21 June 2007).

Revell, P. (2000) Strategic moves, *Sports Teacher*, Spring, 14–15.

Speednet (2000) Primary school physical education – Speednet survey makes depressing reading, *British Journal of Physical Education*, 30(3), 19–20.

Sport England (2003) *Young People and Sport in England. Trends in Participation 1994–2002*. London: Sport England.

STEPS PD (2007) *Fundamental Movement Skills*, Perth, Western Australia: ECURL.

Talbot, M. (2006) Olympic Talent Pool, *Times Educational Supplement*, 3 February.

Times Educational Supplement/Central Council for Physical Recreation (TES/CCPR) (2003) Pupils fail swimming test, *Times Educational Supplement*, 1 August.

Turner-Bissett, R. (2007) Performativity by stealth: a critique of recent initiatives on creativity, *Education 3–13*, 35(2), 193–203.

Warburton, P. (2001) A sporting future for all: fact or fiction, *British Journal of Teaching Physical Education*, 32(2), 18–21.

Ward, H. (2007) Very 1970s: themes make a comeback, *Times Educational Supplement*, 8 June.

Ward, H. and Bloom, A. (2007) Creativity back in favour, *Times Educational Supplement*, 8 June.

Whitehead, M. (2001) The concept of physical literacy, *European Journal of Physical Education*, 6, 127–138.

Williams, E. (1985) Perspectives on Initial Teacher Training in Physical Education for Primary School Teachers, *28th ICHPER World Congress Proceedings*, West London Institute for Higher Education, 726–734.

Woods, P. (2002) Teaching and learning in the new millennium. In C. Day and C. Sugrue (eds) *Developing Teaching and Teachers: International Research Perspectives*. London: Falmer.

Wright, L. (2004) Preserving the value of happiness in primary school Physical Education, *Physical Education and Sport Pedagogy*, 9(2), November 2004, 149–163.

Wyse, D. and Spendlove, D. (2007) Partners in creativity: action research and creative partnerships, *Education 3–13*, 35(2), 181–191.

8

DEFINING AND OPERATIONALISING

Health and well being of primary-aged pupils

Introduction

Not unlike creativity discussed in the previous chapter, the phrase 'health and well being' has become a fashionable addition to our common vocabulary in the twenty-first century. Online searches quickly reveal a plethora of documents at central and local and government level and a number of commercial products (increasingly food) that refer to the phrase. Subjective measures of well being have remained stable in most modern societies for decades (Layard, 2006), so it is unclear exactly why this widespread adoption of the term has emerged so prominently within recent times. Reasons for its use may well be filtered down from a reaction to significant global publications such as the UNICEF 'report card' which ranked the UK in the bottom third of economically advanced nations for child well being (United Nations Children's Fund, 2007). It may also be a useful 'catch all' phrase for politicians and marketers as it is a phrase with seemingly no natural opposite and a phrase that when connected with other language is hard to disagree with, e.g., Do you want health and well being for your family? Yet, oddly, despite the unabated adoption of the phrase there remains significant ambiguity around the definition, usage and function of 'health and well being' in the public policy realm and in the wider world (Ereaut and Whiting, 2008). At a policy level it is the widespread adoption of the term within education which means it cannot be ignored and makes it worthy of attention here. Furthermore, what makes health and well being important to understand is that such terms are socio-cultural constructs and represent a set of meanings that are contested and can therefore change. This chapter will firstly examine what health and well being might mean in an educational sense, before moving on to the ways in which it has been operationalised in both wider policy and curriculum documents.

THOUGHT BOX

So what does health and well being mean to you? Specifically what does primary Physical Education have to offer your vision of health and well being?

So what exactly is health and well being in an educational sense?

In their excellent linguistic analysis of policy documentation, Ereaut and Whiting (2008) identified a complex picture of how 'health and well being' can represent multiple discourses. The first of these is that the phrase is concerned with modern medical thinking. The World Health Organisation first included the words 'well being' in its now famous definition of health in 1946, stating that 'Health is a state of complete physical, mental and social well being and not merely the absence of disease or infirmity' (WHO, 1946: 100). Of interest here is how in common parlance we extract the words 'well being' from this definition of health and then join it back on (as in Health *and* well being), suggesting it means something different or in addition to. The usage of these words in this way is reflective of societal viewpoints seeing 'health' as largely associated with physical health predicated on long standing medical models. The addition of 'well being' therefore represents other aspects, namely psychological and social aspects (Patrick and Erickson, 1993). Policy outcomes from this perspective tend to result in measurement, prescription and referral.

A second related but more nuanced use of the word is its adoption as representation of 'holism' where the physical, psychological and social aspects are part of a wider set of considerations, to which can be added many further aspects such as economic or spiritual (Miller, 2005). This viewpoint sees the interrelationships of these aspects as a whole issue and not something that is easily separated into component parts. As a consequence solutions based on this perspective tend to lead to accusations of government behaving like 'Big Brother' or a 'nanny state' (Pykett, 2010). Some research has been conducted in assessing this holistic picture, the most comprehensive of which in the UK is arguably the report by Gutman and Feinstein (2008). (See Table 8.1)

A third and further evolution on from holism is that of a sustainability discourse. Here communities live within specific limitations as if part of some super holism plan where the wider culture, environment and those within can be sustained to produce a strong, healthy and just society for all, now and in the future (Bonnett, 2002).

A fourth sense in which the word is used within policy documentation represents something of a philosophical desire of what we might like to theoretically achieve. In this form the phrase 'health and well being' conjures a vision of all that is best and desirable and but is no more than an idealised aspiration rather than a real state to be attained or measured. The use of health

TABLE 8.1 Key findings of the Children's Well-Being in Primary School report

Key findings	Explanation
Most children experience positive well being in primary school	Between the ages of 8 and 10, there is an overall increase in levels of well being, with 35 per cent of pupils experiencing improvements. However, 20 per cent suffer from either declining or low levels of well being from 8 to 10 years. This subset is most likely to be male, from low socio-economic status (SES) backgrounds and low achieving.
It is children's individual experiences which mainly affect their well being	It is children's individual experiences such as bullying, victimisation and friendships, and their beliefs about themselves and their environment, which mainly affect their well being, rather than school-level factors such as type of school. There is an element of continuity in these measures; for example, those who experience victimisation at age 8 are more likely than others to experience victimisation at age 10. There is also a high level of interrelatedness within and between the dimensions measured. For example, different forms of antisocial behaviour are associated with one another, but also with poor mental health.
School factors can constitute a measurable difference in a child's well being	School factors explain 3 per cent or less of the variation in pupils' mental health and behaviour, 7 per cent of the variation in Key Stage 2 (age 11) maths scores and 10 per cent of the variation in KS2 English scores. These small, but significant, differences between schools are explained by factors such as school disadvantage and school ethos.
Schools can make a difference for children's well being	Schools make a difference for children's well being, but it is children's individual experiences within schools which are important. Children experience a very different environment, even within the same school, based on their own individual interactions with peers and teachers. This suggests that modifications within individual children's lives are likely to make the most difference to their well being and that child–school 'fit' may be more important for children's well being than attending a particular school.
Socio-demographic factors make little impact	Socio-demographic factors, with the exception of gender, have no effect on children's pro-social and antisocial behaviours, although they do affect school achievement.
Boys have better mental health than girls	Boys have better mental health than girls, with higher levels of belief in their own abilities and more feelings of control. On the other hand, boys are less likely to engage in pro-social, and more likely to engage in antisocial, behaviours.
Much of the variation in children's well being remains unexplained	Much of the variation in children's well being remains unexplained. It is likely that the unmeasured cumulative experiences of children within their home and school are important constituents of their overall well being.

(Adapted from Gutman and Feinstein, 2008)

and well being in this way has its roots in the Greek literature of Aristotle, which led to a Westernised view of what the 'good life' might look like and how we might strive toward it (Robinson, 1999).

If we are to pursue the good life in a consumer driven culture a fifth and final discourse sees the individual take self-responsibility for it. Here well being can be pursued through the adoption of particular skills or traits such as 'resilience' and 'independence' where we can exercise 'lifestyle choice' and practice 'self-help'. This discourse is in keeping with the era of second modernity highlighted in Chapter 2 where a more intense political individualisation has also developed a consumerist and choice driven society which sees less legitimacy in traditional social institutions (Beck and Beck-Gernsheim, 2001). This unabated trend sees people coming to think of themselves as unique individuals, exercising self-consciousness, creativity and agency (Prout, 2000).

Operationalisation of a discourse: ECM and the role for Physical Education

When well being policy has needed to be operationalised, the approach has seen a broad amalgam of all of these influences. In practice, operationalised discourse that results is where the phrase is known, defined and treated as a set of indicators that can measured and achieved. The best example of this in twenty-first-century education policy came following the passing of the Children's Act in 2004 and the publication of *Every Child Matters: Change for Children* (commonly known as ECM), which provided for the first time the legislative structure for developing more effective and accessible services focused around the needs of children, young people and families (DfES, 2004). All those working with children were required to support improvement in five specific outcomes within an operationalised discourse – namely, being healthy; staying safe; enjoying and achieving; making a positive contribution; and achieving economic well being. (See Table 8.2.)

Griggs and Wheeler (2007) identified that the most useful outcomes that could be most effectively addressed through Physical Education and School Sport were those of 'Being Healthy' and 'Making a Positive Contribution', with other outcomes providing natural links at different times. The case for these areas was made in the following way.

'Being healthy'

Engagement in regular physical activity through Physical Education and school sport was thought to have a positive impact on the physical, mental and emotional health of young people:

> Activity in childhood has a range of benefits during childhood which in
> themselves justify the promotion of physical activity for children and

TABLE 8.2 Every Child Matters (DCMS, 2004) – the five outcomes

Outcomes	Indicators to be operationalised
Be healthy	• Physically healthy • Mentally and emotionally healthy • Sexually healthy • Healthy lifestyles • Choose not to take illegal drugs • Parents, carers and families promote healthy choices
Stay safe	• Safe from maltreatment, neglect, violence and sexual exploitation • Safe from accidental injury and death • Safe from bullying and discrimination • Safe from crime and anti-social behaviour in and out of school • Have security, stability and are cared for • Parents, carers and families provide safe homes and stability
Enjoy and achieve	• Ready for school • Attend and enjoy school • Achieve stretching national educational standards at primary school • Achieve personal and social development and enjoy recreation • Achieve stretching national educational standards at secondary school • Parents, carers and families support learning
Make a positive contribution	• Engage in decision-making and support the community and environment • Engage in law-abiding and positive behaviour in and out of school • Develop positive relationships and choose not to bully and discriminate • Develop self-confidence and successfully deal with significant life changes and challenges • Develop enterprising behaviour • Parents, carers and families promote positive behaviour
Achieve economic well being	• Engage in further education, employment or training on leaving school • Ready for employment • Live in decent homes and sustainable communities • Access to transport and material goods • Live in households free from low income • Parents, carers and families are supported to be economically active

young people. These include: healthy growth and development of the musculoskeletal and cardio respiratory systems; maintenance of energy balance (in order to maintain a healthy weight); avoidance of risk factors such as hypertension and high cholesterol; and the opportunity for social interaction, achievement and mental well-being.

(DH, 2004: 2)

With the health risks associated with low levels of participation frequently stressed, both nationally (HEA, 1998; DH, 1999) and internationally (WHO, 1990; USDHHS, 1996), arguably the most important contribution that increased involvement in Physical Education and School Sport can make is by helping to establish a regular habit of participating in physical activity. Not only is this vitally important for young people's current health, but it can provide a stronger platform for the maintenance of good health throughout life. Young people who emerge from their school years feeling confident about their physical skills and bodies, and who have positive experiences of Physical Education and School Sport, are more likely to be active through adulthood (Trudeau et al., 1999; Harro and Riddoch, 2000). Such engagement will also increase knowledge and understanding of how to be healthy and provides an alternative setting in which information on health issues, such as healthy eating, drug taking and teenage pregnancy, can be provided to young people (Sabo et al., 1998; Miller at al., 2000). The combination of positive experiences and increased knowledge facilitates the development of self-confidence among young people, which is empowering by its very nature, demonstrating a strong link between 'Being Healthy' and 'Making a Positive Contribution'.

Make a positive contribution

When schools work to become a central or community focus, as advocated by *Every Child Matters* they also create ideal conditions within which school sport can also flourish. Proactive teachers with responsibility for Physical Education have a real opportunity to be at the forefront of developing a programme of Physical Education and School Sport that engages large numbers of children and adults from across the community in a way that other curriculum areas could not – not least because engagement develops 'social capital' (Bourdieu, 1986) (discussed in more detail in Chapter 9).

Though defining exactly what is meant in practice by social capital can be problematic; the term is perhaps most usefully referred to here as 'the collective value of all "social networks" and the inclinations that arise from these networks to do things for each other' (Putnam, 2000: 3). 'Since sports participation provides a focus for social activity, an opportunity to make friends, develop networks and reduce social isolation, it seems well placed to support the development of social capital' (Bailey, 2005: 77).

A consequence of developing a broad programme of activities (including competitions and festivals) and actively facilitating engagement in Physical Education and School Sport is the creation of a number of opportunities to volunteer (Russell, 2005). Such opportunities enable pupils to develop not only their ability to lead, organise and manage sessions but also contribute to their knowledge and understanding of fitness and health. This in turn may encourage them to adopt a healthier, safer lifestyle, as well as challenging those around them to do the same. By pursuing opportunities to volunteer and work towards related schemes and awards, it is argued that confidence is raised, pupils improve their ability to develop good relationships, respect others and be responsible for their actions, therefore making a positive contribution. More broadly, what volunteering does is provide 'young people a stake in their communities, helping them to make sense of their relationship to the world around them' (Russell, 2005: 23). This stake makes young people feel valued and gives them a platform from which their voice can be heard and through engagement in sport many 'hard to reach' young people feel they can contribute (Home Office, 2003).

This latter point is of particular significance when considering that research indicates that extended engagement in regular sports activities has been shown to strengthen some of the protective factors (leaders and coaches leading by example, social bonding and opportunities for developing social and reasoning skills) and weaken some of the risk factors (community disorganisation, alienation, a lack of social commitment and attitudes that condone offending) which influence rates of youth offending (YJB, 2001; ODPM/YJB/DCMS, 2005). Sport has been shown to be a useful 'hook' in situations where school transition, difficult social situations and low expectations have been identified as significant concerns. The 'Playing for Success' initiative is one such example whereby study support centres have been set up in professional football clubs and other venues, using sport as the medium to support core curriculum work, such as literacy and numeracy (DfES/NFER, 2003). Though the contribution sport makes in this instance is somewhat indirect, its ability to attract participants in the first place, maintain their interest in education and engage with organisations within their community should not be underestimated.

Operationalising a curriculum for health and well being: from ECM to Rose to Curriculum for excellence

As explained in Chapter 3, after almost a decade of the twenty-first century, the Labour Government commissioned Sir Jim Rose, former director of inspection at Ofsted, to head up a review of the primary curriculum In England. In April 2009, what has commonly been referred to as the 'Rose Review' was published (DCSF, 2009) (see the extracts in Box 8.1). Here Physical Education was located under a holistic looking umbrella of 'Understanding Physical Development, Health and Well Being'.

BOX 8.1 ROSE REVIEW – EXTRACTS FROM THE PROPOSED UNIT FOR UNDERSTANDING PHYSICAL DEVELOPMENT, HEALTH AND WELL BEING (DCSF, 2009)

Learning in this area should include an appropriate balance of focused subject teaching and well-planned opportunities to use, apply and develop knowledge and skills across the whole curriculum.

Curriculum aims

This area of learning contributes to the curriculum aims for all young people to become:
• successful learners who enjoy learning, make progress and achieve;
• confident individuals who are able to live safe, healthy and fulfilling lives;
• responsible citizens who make a positive contribution to society.

Why is this area of learning important?

To enjoy healthy, active and fulfilling lives, children must learn to respond positively to challenges, to recognise and manage risk and to develop their self-confidence and physical capabilities. Such learning lays the foundations for long-term well being and contributes to children's mental, social, emotional economic and physical development.

They learn about their changing bodies and the importance of nutrition and rest, helping them make informed choices and lead healthy, balanced lifestyles. Through enjoyable physical activities, they learn to increase body control, coordination and dexterity. Children learn about their responsibilities both as individuals and members of groups and about what is right and wrong. They learn to compete fairly and to cooperate as individuals and in groups and teams, understanding their own and others' roles. As their confidence grows, they become more enterprising and financially capable, finding new ways of doing things and developing a positive attitude to seeking solutions. Children develop a growing self-awareness and a commitment to self-improvement so they can make informed decisions that lead to happier and healthier lives. They raise their aspirations, set goals and work to achieve them, seeing how this will influence opportunities in education, leisure, the world of work and their quality of life.

1. Essential knowledge

Children should build secure knowledge of the following:
a.   healthy living depends upon a balance of physical activity, nutrition, leisure, work and rest to promote well being;
b.   physical competence and performance can be improved through

practice, control and dexterity as well as creative thinking and commitment;

c. good interpersonal relationships promote personal well being and are sustained through a positive sense of personal identity and respect for similarities and differences;

d. personal well being depends upon high aspirations and the development of financial and enterprise capability;

e. challenge and risk can be managed through well-informed choices that lead to safe, full and active lives.

2. Key skills

These are the skills that children need to learn to make progress:

• reflect on and evaluate evidence when making personal choices or bringing about improvements in performance and behaviour;

• generate and implement ideas, plans and strategies, exploring alternatives;

• move with ease, poise, stability and control in a range of physical contexts;

• find information and check its accuracy including the different ways that issues are presented by different viewpoints and media;

• communicate clearly and interact with a range of audiences to express views on issues that affect their well being.

3. Breadth of learning

a. Children should be taught knowledge, skills and understanding they need to help them achieve physical, mental, intellectual, social, emotional and economic well being.

b. Children should learn about the importance of healthy lifestyles. They should participate in a range of activities that promote physical skilfulness and development through indoor and outdoor activities including creative play. They should take part in physical activities that involve competing with and outwitting opponents, accurate replication of actions, optimum performance and creative problem solving. Children should be able to swim a minimum distance of 25 metres and refine skills within aerobic activities and ball games. As a result of taking part in activities, they should be able to identify what types of physical activities they enjoy and find out how to get involved. They should learn about the importance of healthy lifestyles and have opportunities to prepare and cook simple balanced meals. They learn how nutrition, exercise and hygiene contribute to their well being.

c.   Children should learn about the physical and emotional changes that take place as they grow. They learn about relationships and sex within the context of caring and stable relationships. They should learn how to make decisions that promote and sustain better physical, mental and emotional health. They should learn how to manage their emotions and develop and sustain relationships, recognising diversity and respecting themselves and others. Through a range of activities and experiences, children should have opportunities to collaborate and to compete individually, in pairs, groups and teams. Through these activities, they learn about their capabilities, their limitations and their potential.

d.   Children develop a growing awareness of the adult world recognising that there is a range of work that people do and a variety of ways that people contribute to society. They should learn how education and training can improve their opportunities in later life. To raise their aspirations, children should have opportunities to meet people from a range of occupations as well as attend events outside of school. They should learn about where money comes from, its uses and how to manage it. They should have opportunities to develop and use enterprise skills.

e.   Children should learn how to solve problems, to embrace and overcome challenges and deal with change. They should learn about staying safe and how to identify and manage risks relating to issues including harmful relationships, drugs and alcohol, and how and where to get help.

Proposed curriculum progression: Physical Education

Early

E8.   To develop control and coordination of their physical movements.

E9.   To recognise, observe and apply rules in competitive and cooperative games and other physical activities and why they are important.

E10. To devise and use repeat compositions sequences in physical activities.

E11. To use and apply simple tactics and strategies.

E12. To improve performance by observation and use criteria for evaluation.

E13. About the benefits of regular exercise and how their bodies feel when they exercise.

Middle

M9.   To control and coordinate their bodies and movements with increasing skill and confidence.

M10. To follow and apply more complex rules in range of competitive and cooperative games and physical activities.

M11. To develop physical skills and techniques through observation, evaluation and refinement; and to use repetition and practice to reach higher standards.

M12. To use tactics, strategies and compositional ideas to achieve set objectives and improve performance.

M13. To recognise ways in which stamina and flexibility can be improved through daily physical activity.

Late

L11. To perform physical movements and complex series of movements with increasing control, coordination, precision and consistency.

L12. To create and apply rules and use more complex compositions, tactics and strategies in competitive and cooperative games and other physical activities.

L13. To develop and perform sequences and compositions using appropriate movements to express ideas and emotions.

L14. To refine physical skills and techniques commenting on strengths and weaknesses in their own and others' performance.

L15. To recognise the benefits of practice and reflection for improving personal and group performance.

L16. To understand the particular benefits of different physical activities for promoting health.

Furthermore, specific activities such as Dance were given greater focus under another heading of 'Understanding the Arts'. Clear synergies were also apparent between the Rose Review and the underpinning EYFS strategy. However with the coming to power of the Coalition government in 2010 all such plans were scrapped and the opportunity for Operationalising a holistic curriculum with Health and Well Being at its core was lost – in England at least.

By contrast, Scotland's 'Curriculum for Excellence' strategy has made a concerted effort to provide a more coherent, flexible and enriched curriculum from 3 to 18. Launched in 2010/11, the curriculum is laid out in eight major areas: Expressive Arts, Health and Well Being, Languages, Mathematics, Religious and Moral Education, Sciences, Social Studies and Technologies. Of relevance here 'Physical Education, Physical Activity and Sport' can be located in the area of Health and Well Being, along with five other topics: Mental, Emotional, Social and Physical Well Being, Planning for Choices and Changes, Food and Health, Substance Misuse, and Relationships, Sexual Health and Parenthood (LTS, 2009) (See Table 8.3.)

TABLE 8.3 Physical Education extracts from the Curriculum for Excellence (LTS, 2009)

Physical Education, Physical Activity and Sport

Physical Education

Physical education provides learners with a platform from which they can build physical competences, improve aspects of fitness, and develop personal and interpersonal skills and attributes. It enables learners to develop the concepts and skills necessary for participation in a wide range of physical activity, sport, dance and outdoor learning, and enhances their physical well being in preparation for leading a fulfilling, active and healthy lifestyle.

They encounter a variety of practical learning experiences, including working on their own, with a partner and in small and large groups, and using small and large equipment and apparatus, both outdoors and indoors.

Learning in, through and about physical education is enhanced by participating on a regular basis in a wide range of purposeful, challenging, progressive and enjoyable physical activities with choice built in for all learners. The Scottish Government expects schools to continue to work towards the provision of at least two hours of good quality physical education for every child, every week.

	Early	First	Second	Third	Fourth
Movement skills, competencies and concepts	I am learning to move my body well, exploring how to manage and control it and finding out how to use and share space. HWB 0-21a	I am discovering ways that I can link actions and skills to create movement patterns and sequences. This has motivated me to practise and improve my skills to develop control and flow. HWB 1-21a	As I encounter new challenges and contexts for learning, I am encouraged and supported to demonstrate my ability to select, adapt and apply movement skills and strategies, creatively, accurately and with control. HWB 2-21a/HWB 3-21a	As I encounter new challenges and contexts for learning, I am encouraged and supported to demonstrate my ability to select, adapt and apply movement skills and strategies, creatively, accurately and with control. HWB 2-21a/HWB 3-21a	As I encounter a variety of challenges and contexts for learning, I am encouraged and supported to demonstrate my ability to select and apply a wide range of complex movement skills and strategies, creatively, accurately and with consistency and control. HWB 4-21a

continued …

Table 8.3 continued

	Early	First	Second	Third	Fourth
	I am developing my movement skills through practice and energetic play. HWB 0-22a	I am developing skills and techniques and improving my level of performance and fitness. HWB 1-22a	I practise, consolidate and refine my skills to improve my performance. I am developing and sustaining my levels of fitness. HWB 2-22a /HWB 3-22a	I practise, consolidate and refine my skills to improve my performance. I am developing and sustaining my levels of fitness. HWB 2-22a /HWB 3-22a	I can organise my time to practise, consolidate and refine my skills to achieve my highest quality performance in a range of contexts. I am developing and sustaining my level of performance across all aspects of fitness. HWB 4-22a
Cooperation and competition	I am aware of my own and others' needs and feelings especially when taking turns and sharing resources. I recognise the need to follow rules. HWB 0-23a	I can follow and understand rules and procedures, developing my ability to achieve my personal goals. I recognise and can adopt different roles in a range of practical activities. HWB 1-23a	While working and learning with others, I improve my range of skills, demonstrate tactics and achieve identified goals. HWB 2-23a	I am developing the skills to lead and recognise strengths of group members, including myself. I contribute to groups and teams through my knowledge of individual strengths, group tactics, and strategies. HWB 3-23a	While learning together, and in leadership situations, I can: experience different roles and take responsibility in organising a physical event contribute to a supportive and inclusive environment demonstrate behaviour that contributes to fair play. HWB 4-23a

| Evaluating and appreciating | By exploring and observing movement, I can describe what I have learned about it.
HWB 0-24a | I can recognise progress and achievement by discussing my thoughts and feelings and giving and accepting feedback.
HWB 1-24a | By reflecting on my own and others' work and evaluating it against shared criteria, I can recognise improvement and achievement and use this to progress further.
HWB 2-24a | I can analyse and discuss elements of my own and others' work, recognising strengths and identifying areas where improvements can be made.
HWB 3-24a | I can:
observe closely, reflect, describe and analyse key aspects of my own and others' performances
make informed judgements, specific to an activity
monitor and take responsibility for improving my own performance based on recognition of personal strengths and development needs.
HWB 4-24a |

Physical Activity and Sport

In addition to planned physical education sessions, physical activity and sport take place in the classroom, in the school, during travel such as walking and cycling, in the outdoor environment and in the community. Learning in, through and about physical activity and sport is enhanced by participating in a wide range of purposeful and enjoyable physical pursuits at break times, lunchtimes, within and beyond the place of learning.

The experiences and outcomes are intended to establish a pattern of daily physical activity which, research has shown, is most likely to lead to sustained physical activity in adult life. Experiences and outcomes should also open up opportunities for learners to participate and perform at their highest level in sport and, if interested, pursue careers in the health and leisure industries.

continued …

Table 8.3 continued

Early	First	Second	Third	Fourth
I am enjoying daily opportunities to participate in different kinds of energetic play, both outdoors and indoors. HWB 0-25a	Within and beyond my place of learning I am enjoying daily opportunities to participate in physical activities and sport, making use of available indoor and outdoor space. HWB 1-25a	I am experiencing enjoyment and achievement on a daily basis by taking part in different kinds of energetic physical activities of my choosing, including sport and opportunities for outdoor learning, available at my place of learning and in the wider community. HWB 2-25a / HWB 3-25a		I continue to enjoy daily participation in moderate to vigorous physical activity and sport and can demonstrate my understanding that it can: contribute to and promote my learning develop my fitness and physical and mental well being develop my social skills, positive attitudes and values make an important contribution to living a healthy lifestyle. HWB 4-25a
		I have investigated the role of sport and the opportunities it may offer me. I am able to access opportunities for participation in sport and the development of my performance in my place of learning and beyond. HWB 2-26a / HWB 3-26a		I can explain the role of sport in cultural heritage and have explored the opportunities available for me to participate in school sport and sporting events. I make use of participation and performance pathways that allow me to continue and extend my sporting experience in my place of learning and beyond. HWB 4-26a

The major implications for physical education within health and well being agendas

Though there have been increasingly regular publications which support broad moves of Physical Education to be developmental, holistic and to have a focus towards goals of lifelong physical activity and health and well being (see YST/SE/CSPn/afPE/scUK, 2013) there is still a reservation for some that Physical Education must somehow stand alone if it is to make a contribution to the learning of pupils. For example, in England, afPE were in opposition to Physical Education being subsumed within the holistic-looking umbrella of 'Understanding Physical Development, Health and Well Being' proposed by the Rose Review. The association feared a lack of subject identity and foresaw the eventual removal of the subject from the curriculum (Vaughan, 2009). In Scotland, Woodhead (2009) claimed that CfE is built upon 'hopelessly utopian goals' and that shared holistic agendas confuse what should be the primary importance of subject knowledge in teaching. In addition, Her Majesty's Inspectorate of Education (2008) recommended that Physical Education should not become overly recreational in its reconnection with holistic ideals but should promote instead learning which is more explanatory with regards to the principles underpinning performance. Thorburn et al. (2011) indicate that in any move of Physical Education towards and within health and well being agendas teachers must be able to design and implement authentic learning opportunities which are not stifled or contrived.

THOUGHT BOX

Can Physical Education exist within broader agendas of health and well being without losing its identity? What are the implications for practitioners if the sole focus of primary Physical Education was the health and well being of the child?

Conclusion

Global and national agendas which move towards health and well being look set to say in the foreground for some time to come. In different places and different times they have the potential to influence significant policy documents such as school curricula. However as long as words like health and well being represent a set of meanings that are contested, their interpretation and operationalisation will vary enormously. Primary Physical Education has the potential to provide secure foundations for holistic curriculum models such as the Curriculum for Excellence in Scotland (see Jess and Collins, 2003). However moves which ally Physical Education to health and well being agendas will not be without their problems as discussed earlier in the chapter, 'especially as such a change has far reaching implications for the dominant performance-oriented curriculum with its accompanying behaviourist inclined pedagogical approaches' (Thorburn et al., 2011: 393).

KEY READINGS

To further understand the intricacies of the phrase well being and how it has become manifest within policy documentation a good starting point would be Ereaut, G. and Whiting, R. (2008). *What do we mean by 'well being'?: and why might it matter?* (London: DCSF). To see how well being has been operationalised at a curriculum level, understanding the landscape in Scotland would be a useful case study. For policy documentation, The Curriculum for Excellence is available online at www.educationscotland.gov.uk/thecurriculum/whatiscurriculumforexcellence/index.asp. Those wishing to understand the complexities and challenges of its implementation should find Thorburn, M., Jess, M. and Atencio, M. (2011) Thinking differently about curriculum: analysing the potential contribution of physical education as part of 'health and wellbeing' during a time of revised curriculum ambitions in Scotland, *Physical Education and Sport Pedagogy*, 16(4), 383–398.

References

Bailey, R. (2005) Evaluating the relationship between Physical Education, sport and social inclusion, *Educational Review*, 57(1), 71–90.

Beck, U. and Beck-Gernsheim, E. (2001) *Individualization*. London: Sage.

Bonnett, M. (2002) Education for sustainability as a frame of mind, *Environmental Education Research*, 8(1), 9–20.

Bourdieu, P. (1986) *The Forms of Capital*. Cambridge, MA: Routledge and Kegan Paul.

Department for Children, Schools and Families (DCSF) (2009) *Independent Review of the Primary Curriculum: Final Report* (*The Rose Review*). London: DCSF.

Department for Education and Skills/National Foundation for Education Research (DfES/NFER) (2003) *The Playing for Success Initiative: An Evaluation of the Fourth Year*. London: DfES.

Department of Health (DH) (1999) *Saving Lives: Our Healthier Nation*. London: DH.

Department of Health (DH) (2004) *Chief Medical Office Report: At Least Five a Week – Evidence on the Impact of Physical Activity and Its Relationship to Health*. London: DH.

Department for Education and Skills (DfES) (2004) *Every Child Matters: Change for Children*. London: DfES.

Ereaut, G. and Whiting, R. (2008) *What do we mean by 'wellbeing'? and why might it matter?* London: DCSF.

Griggs, G. and Wheeler, K. (2007) 'Play up, play up and play the game': the implications of *Every Child Matters* within physical education and school sport, *Education 3–13*, 35(3), 273–282.

Gutman, L. and Feinstein, L. (2008). *Children's well-being in primary school: Pupil and school effects*. London: Centre for Research on the Wider Benefits of Learning, Institute of Education, University of London.

Harro, M. and Riddoch, C. (2000) Physical activity. In N. Armstrong and W. van Mechelen (eds) *Physical Exercise Science and Medicine*. Oxford: Oxford University Press.

Health Education Authority (HEA) (1998) *Young and Active? Young People and Health-Enhancing Physical Activity, Evidence and Implications*. London: HEA.

Her Majesty's Inspectorate of Education (2008) *Physical Education: A Portrait of Current Practice in Scottish Schools and Pre-school Centres*. Available online at www.hmie.gov.uk/documents/publication/pepcp.html (accessed 12 January 2010).

Home Office (2003) *Citizenship Survey*. London: Home Office.

Jess, M. and Collins, D. (2003) Primary physical education in Scotland: the future in the making, *European Journal of Physical Education*, 8, 103–118.

Layard, R. (2006) Happiness and public policy: a challenge to the profession, *The Economic Journal*, 116(510), 24–33.

Learning and Teaching Scotland (LTS) (2009) *Curriculum for Excellence*. Edinburgh: LTS.

Miller, J.P. (ed.) (2005) *Holistic Learning and Spirituality in Education: Breaking New Ground*. Albany, NY: SUNY Press.

Miller, K.E., Sabo, D.F., Melnick, M.J., Farrell, M.P. and Barnes, G.M. (2000) *The Women's Sports Foundation Report: Health Risks and the Teen Athlete*. East Meadow, NY: Women's Sports Foundation.

Office of the Deputy Prime Minister, Youth Justice Board, Department of Culture, Media and Sport and Sport England (ODPM/YJB/DCMS) (2005) Sports Activities and Youth Offending – Joint Paper. London, ODPM/YJB/DCMS/Sport England.

Patrick, D.L. and Erickson, P. (1993) *Health Status and Health Policy: Quality of Life in Health Care Evaluation and Resource*. Oxford: Oxford University Press.

Prout, A. (2000) Children's participation: control and self-realisation in British late modernity, *Children and Society*, 14, 304–315.

Putnam, R.D. (2000) *Bowling Alone*. New York: Touchstone.

Pykett, J. (2010) Citizenship education and narratives of pedagogy, *Citizenship Studies*, 14(6), 621–635.

Robinson, D. (1999) *Aristotle's Psychology*. New York: POLOS

Russell, I.M. (2005) *A National Framework for Youth Action and Engagement – The Russell Commission Report*. London: TSO.

Sabo, D., Miller, K., Farrell, M., Barnes, G. and Melnick, M. (1998) *The Women's Sports Foundation Report: Sport and Teen Pregnancy*. East Meadow, NY: Women's Sports Foundation.

Thorburn, M., Jess, M. and Atencio, M. (2011). Thinking differently about curriculum: analysing the potential contribution of physical education as part of 'health and wellbeing' during a time of revised curriculum ambitions in Scotland, *Physical Education and Sport Pedagogy*, 16(4), 383–398.

Trudeau, F., Laurencelle, L., Tremblay, J., Rajic, M. and Shephard, R.J. (1999) Daily primary school Physical Education: effects on physical activity during adult life, *Medicine and Science in Sports and Exercise*, 31, 338–342.

United Nations Children's Fund (UNICEF) (2007) *Child Poverty in Perspective: An Overview of Child Well-being in Rich Countries* (No. inreca07/19). UNICEF Innocenti Research Centre.

US Department of Health and Human Services (USDHHS) (1996) *Physical Activity and Health: A Report of the Surgeon General*. Atlanta, GA: Centers for Disease Control.

Vaughan, R. (2009) Plea to keep PE off the sidelines. *TES online.* Available online at www. tes.co.uk/article.aspx?storycode=6013452 (accessed 18 May 2010).

Woodhead, C. (2009) When will they ever learn?. *The Sunday Times*, April 12. Available online at www.timesonline.co.uk/tol/news/uk/scotland/article6077611.ece (accessed 18 May 2010).

World Health Organization (WHO) (1946) Preamble to the constitution of the World Health Organization as adopted by the International Health Conference, New York, 19–22 June 1946.

World Health Organization (WHO) (1990) *Prevention in Childhood of Adult Cardiovascular Diseases: Time for Action*. Geneva: WHO.

Youth Justice Board (YJB) (2001) *Communities that Care: Risk and Protective Factors Associated with Youth Crime and Effective Interventions to Prevent It*. London: YJB.

Youth Sport Trust (YST)/Sport England (SE)/County Sport Partnership Network (CSPn)/Association for Physical Education (afPE)/Sports Coach UK (scUK) (2013) Primary School Physical Literacy Framework. Available online at www.afpe.org.uk/images/stories/Physical_Literacy_Framework_Final.pdf (accessed 6 January 2014).

9

UNDERSTANDING THE TRINITY WITHIN PRIMARY PHYSICAL EDUCATION

Gender, social class and ethnicity

Introduction

Engagement in physical activity is patterned by gender, social class and ethnicity (Sport England, 2003). During the course of a person's life there are many broad influences upon physical activity behaviour which include intra-personal, social and environmental factors (Sallis and Owen, 1999). However much of the major influences and choices can be traced back to our experiences during the primary years of schooling. This may seem less obvious on face value but the fact remains that the curriculum is not taught to pupils or taught by teachers who live in a vacuum and thus examining issues concerning gender, social class and ethnicity provides valuable lenses with which to examine and explain the decisions that we make. To fully understand some of these complex issues this chapter will provide relevant historical background details.

Examining gender: the significance of the Victorian legacy

The origins of contemporary sport were developed in a period between the mid-nineteenth century and early twentieh century in both Britain and North America (Guttmann, 1994). In particular, boys' public schools provided the setting for the development of institutionalised and codified team games where the moral benefits of 'playing the game' were professed (Mangan, 1981; Holt, 1989). In particular, team games such as cricket and rugby were seen as fundamental to the curriculum and were perceived as enabling the building of one's character and the teaching of characteristics such as manliness and loyalty – qualities that were seen as 'transferable to the world beyond' (McIntosh, 1979: 27). What is referred to as the 'cult of athleticism' involved training young men to be leaders and became the cornerstone of the Muscular Christianity movement, which professed the positive moral benefits of physical exercise and sport (Mangan, 1981; McIntosh, 1987). This became enshrined in popular romantic sporting mythology embodied in such texts as *Tom Brown's Schooldays* (Rees and Miracle, 2000). In particular the 'cult of athleticism' reflected a very specific image of Victorian masculinity, which while celebrating physical prowess prized the ideal of gentlemanly conduct embodied in amateurism (Hargreaves, 1994). Significantly 'games playing in the boys' public schools provided the dominant image of masculine identity in sports and a model for their future development in Britain and throughout the world' (Hargreaves, 1994: 43).

The early twentieth century saw the continued rapid expansion of professional sport, including the slower development and innovation of women's sport rooted in the English middle classes (Tranter, 1998). With the latter came both the loosening and the reinforcement of Victorian gendered discourses. Heated debate raged among physical educators and the medical profession about whether physical activity was in fact beneficial to health or dangerous to the fragile female form (Theberge, 2000). Significantly, the debate was resolved by the introduction of modified activities that were less strenuous and were therefore considered more suited to women – e.g. running shorter distances in athletics (Cahn, 1995). However, the adoption of such a model served to reinforce the Victorian ideals and myths of female frailty and a dominant view of femininity which became entrenched in the culture of many sports (Mangan, 1981). These were largely imposed by men and internalised by middle class women inculcated with bourgeois norms, serving only to confirm the 'natural' differences between the sexes (Theberge, 1989; Hargreaves, 1994). These associations largely continue today through modern competitive sport (Connell, 1987). An obvious example of how this practice continues is the disparity still found in elite tennis where men play five-set matches and women play only three-set matches in grand slam events. Because events such as these are the most prestigious and attract more TV coverage and visibility, this only serves to reinforce an image of 'culturally exalted masculinity' via sport (Connell, 1995: 77). Within primary schools these associations are manifest within Physical Education and school sport and are most easily seen when considering gender appropriateness.

Examining gender: the legacy of gender appropriateness

Many writings within Physical Education concerning the curriculum on offer indicate that traditional sporting programmes are still dominant (Capel, 2007; Griggs and Ward, 2012). In many secondary schools Physical Education is delivered in single-sex groupings and has indoor and outdoor activities dependent on the season (Flintoff and Scraton, 2001). These are typically delivered along gender appropriated lines (Leaman, 1984) – for example, the boys participated in football, basketball and rugby for the majority of their games programme while the girls participated in netball and hockey for a bulk of theirs. These circumstances confirm Capel's (2007: 495) assessment that 'physical education in the majority of schools looks very similar. There seems to be an implicit agreement as to what should be included in the curriculum and how it should be taught.' Within primary schools single-sex groupings remain the exception rather than the rule within Physical Education lessons; however, the gender appropriateness of activities is still evident in extra-curricular provision where girls and boys replicate the pattern evident within secondary schooling (Green, 2008; Sport England, 2003). The apparent keenness for parents and teachers for girls and boys to conform to gender-appropriate behaviours is well established including the colours of clothes in which we dress our children to the activities in which we encourage them to participate (Horne et al, 1999). Much of this landscape is further amplified by the media where everything we consume has been chosen for us by those making editorial decisions. For example, though the amount of coverage women achieved in the last decade or so, compared to the middle or late twentieth century, has increased significantly, a worldwide underrepresentation of women persists (Pressland and Griggs, 2014). Investigation into this point reveals the media's reproduction of dominant images of masculinity and femininity. Sports which emphasise physical strength, speed and the use of force are given the most coverage and attract the most money. However, they are also the major sites where traditional notions of masculinity are portrayed making it hard for women to access. Where women are given coverage tends to be when engaged in activities which are deemed gender appropriate and reinforcing traditional images of femininity emphasising elements such as grace and aesthetics (Duncan and Messner, 1998). Coverage is less often seen which contradicts these viewpoints, hence the absence in the daily media of activities such as women's boxing.

While it has been established many girls want to be physically active, a tension remains between wishing to appear feminine and thus attractive and the sweaty muscular image attached to active women (Cockburn and Clarke, 2002). For females, pressure to conform to dominant feminine discourses such as popular ideals of beauty remain important reasons for teenage girls being physically active. In particular research has revealed that engagement in physical activity is largely driven by concerns about body shape and weight management among many young women (Porter, 2002). Key transition points such as that from childhood to adulthood have been identified as key risk times for drop-out. Teenagers in particular wish to disassociate themselves from 'childish' activities instead preferring to choose activities that were independent and conferred a more adult identity (Coakley and White, 1992). Research has also indicated that the increasing pressure on children to 'grow up' earlier and the increasing sexualisation of young people encourages primary-aged pupils to conform to these adult perceptions earlier and earlier (Horne, et al., 1999). Therefore key to maintaining participation in physical activity, and particularly during key transitional phases, is support from significant others. Those who continue to participate through these transitionary periods such as changing schools highlight the importance of positive influences of those around them (Flintoff and Scraton, 2001).

Examining gender: the legacy on training

More recent research has indicated that the key problem of disengagement lies within the curriculum and the pedagogic content (Rich, 2003, 2004; Sandford and Rich, 2006). Many girls appear disenchanted with traditional, gender-appropriate Physical Education programmes such as those including netball and hockey (Paechter, 2003). Teacher training experiences remain gendered with little time to reflect and acknowledge (Flintoff and Scraton, 2006). Only by developing a critical understanding can this cycle be broken (Stidder et al., 2012). Consequently studies have begun to research the development of alternative curricula designs in a bid to facilitate girls' re-engagement with Physical Education programmes (Griffiths and Griggs, 2008).

As has already been discussed in Chapter 4, the cycle of student preparation within primary schooling is continually reinforced by mentors who lack time to adequately confront such issues (Morgan and Bourke, 2005, 2008; Stroot and Ko, 2006). As such many teachers revert to their own personal experiences of secondary schooling and sports participation (Capel, 2007) which, as has been discussed, is laden with gendered discourses. One further illustration of this is the difference in teaching styles identified and fostered between male and female teachers delivering Physical Education, with men shown to deliver using more reproductive approaches, such as command and practice styles (Green, 2008; Hargreaves, 1994).

THOUGHT BOX

Consider all aspects of practice espoused by yourself or others. Which decisions can you identify as being influenced by gender? How easy would it be to change one of these elements?

Social class

Social class is largely an economically grounded concept (Sugden and Tomlinson, 2002) and though at face value may appear to many unfashionable and not relevant (Bairner, 2007), to primary Physical Education and school sport experiences its impact cannot be underestimated. Though social class as a category can be hard to define for many, it remains a 'visceral reality constituted by a set of affectively loaded, social and economic relationships that are likely to strongly influence, if not determine and dominate people's lives' (Evans and Bairner, 2012: 142). It is evident in different social sites or fields (Bourdieu, 1986), particularly in work, families and schools (Roberts and Brodie, 1992). In order to better understand class divisions it is useful to consider how the different social, cultural and physical dimensions can be identified (Collins and Kay, 2003). It is to these ideas this chapter now moves.

Understanding capital: a useful tool

To talk about someone's capital in common parlance refers to their economic wealth. We might consider how much capital someone has to invest or what the return might be on their capital for a particular venture. Different theorists have suggested that other forms of capital exist in which we can invest and in which, beyond the economic, can be thought of as 'rich'. The first of these is 'social capital' (Field, 2003) and includes the social relationships we develop with people such as our friends and colleagues. A good illustration of this is to watch and study any primary school playground. The chances are that the most active children have a high degree of social capital as they create games and activities to which they invite others to join. In turn they too are invited to join in the play of others and as this occurs the social capital of all involved grows. Children who possess less social capital invariably choose not to instigate such physical play and, should they do so, it is less likely that those with highest social capital would choose to join them (to use an economic argument such children might be seen as a 'bad' investment at this stage). The implications of this of course spiral as the most physically active children on the playground may well gain both increased competence and confidence, and take this to other settings such as Physical Education lessons and after school clubs. In a transactional sense what these children have done is to use their social capital to create physical activity and, by developing their competence, invest in their 'physical capital'.

Physical capital as a concept comprises the physical things that you can do or know about (McDonald, 2003). Though it is arguably a component of what has been termed 'cultural capital', which pertains to the wider skills, knowledge and values that we acquire during our social experiences (Bourdieu, 1984), it is worthy of specific distinction when examining areas such as Physical Education which contain contrasts of bodily practices. Differences in primary school are most easily seen in instances where the gender appropriate activities outlined earlier in this chapter remain unchallenged. For example, an eleven year-old boy who plays football as his principal activity of choice during school, after school and at home has invested a considerable amount of time and energy over the years in developing his physical competency in this activity. By contrast a girl who has been led to believe that football is not an appropriate game in which to take part will not have invested anywhere near that amount of time or energy in the same activity. Consequently the two children in that example possess quite different amount of physical capital pertaining to football and possibly many other areas of physical activity too. Again the chances are these gaps will widen as further time passes. Physical capital can also be bought. Economic capital can be traded in a classic sense as money can be handed over for such things as swimming lessons. Years of swimming lessons after school on a particular night of the week through the primary years sees an eleven year-old child likely to gain a significant competency level. In areas identified as having higher socio-economic status more parents will pay for their children to partake in such lessons and by contrast in areas identified as having lower socio-economic status, parents will not. Children from different areas feeding into the same secondary school then raise some interest challenges and searching questions. For example which children are gifted and talented? In some instances is it those parents who have paid the most? Another interest point here is that the physical or body related aspects of capital further cement and illustrate an individual social class (Kirk, 2004). Although not impossible, a budding rower, fencer or lacrosse player, for example, is more likely to emerge from public fee-paying schools as these activities are more readily taught and practised in these environments than anywhere else. By contrast, the majority of boxing champions grew up and were schooled in quite different surroundings. Though not all the activities we engage in after the age of eleven were undertaken before that age, the choices that we subsequently make are highly conditioned by this time period.

Having obtained greater physical capital also has a positive effect upon a person's health, as they are more likely continue to enjoy doing the physical activity (thus exercising) for a longer period of their life. Those who live in areas of higher socio-economic status who continually invest economic capital into their leisure time and that of their children unsurprisingly are shown to take part in more physical activity (Duncan et al., 2004; Linder, 2002; Wright et al., 2003). By contrast there remain strong links between areas of low socio-economic status and high levels of inactivity, obesity and smoking (RCP, 2004; Wanless, 2004). Children living and being schooled in such areas face real challenges in order to break long-standing cycles of cultural reproduction that limit their creation of capital both now and into the future. Studies comparing schools in contrasting bands of socio-economic status underline the dividing practices that occur both during curricular Physical Education and after school provision (Wright and Burrows, 2006; Dagkas and Stathi, 2007). Emphasis on the importance of physical activity and participation in Physical Education was shown to be different in terms of educational context and provision, leading to the conclusion that 'differences in ability are demonstrably associated with social class' (Wright and Burrows, 2006: 277).

THOUGHT BOX

What are the benefits and risks of introducing an activity within Physical Education and school sport that is perceived to sit within a different social class than the children and their families?

Separating race and ethnicity

The term 'race' remains widespread within sporting contexts but as a concept it lacks both relevance and validity, as it is based upon superficial and observable physical differences such as skin colour (Harrison and Belcher, 2006). Furthermore, in a globalised world with increasing migration, populations become further mixed and thus blurring any supposed meaningful subdivision. By contrast the term 'ethnicity' is much more useful, focusing on the cultural tradition and heritage with which a particular group of people identify (Coakley, 2008). Consequently belonging to a particular ethnic group is 'best viewed in terms of shared social experiences rather than shared genetic material' (Green, 2008: 168). Thus the concept of ethnicity helps us to make sense of the processes by which particular ethnic groups learn to create particular identities.

Ethnicity and Physical Education

Little has been written specifically about the relationship between ethnicity and Physical Education and almost nothing has been written pertaining to the primary age phase. Writings tend to be confined to global points about race, ethnicity and sport or case studies focused upon secondary school environments. Of relevance to select from such sources are the claims that are often made of the role that Physical Education and school sport can play in integrating ethnic minority groups into dominant cultures (Green, 2008). However academic studies have typically found that rather than breaking down barriers, Physical Education and school sport opportunities serve to reinforce stereotypes (Coakley, 2008) and 'maintain and fortify ethnic boundaries' (Fleming, 1991: 176). Specific examples can be seen in studies where teachers actively encourage Afro-Caribbean children into participation of particular activities (and even specific positions in sports teams) and at the same time dismiss their academic potential (Carroll, 1998; Cashmore, 2005; Jarvie, 1991).

In ethnic minority groups where physical activity is not considered a significant cultural practice, Physical Education lessons are the only opportunity to engage children in a physical setting. Within these settings, primary schools provide a vital role in develop basic motor competencies to underpin more complex movements needed in later life. Failure to do so leads to the development of restricted movement opportunities, the reinforcement of stereotypes and impacts upon any potential future lifelong physical activity (Fleming, 1991). In order to engage young people from increasingly diverse populations the selection of activity is also of significance and failure to understand this leads to conflict (Carroll, 1998). Studies show that those who seek to uphold well-established Physical Education traditions and practices within schools continue to see children from ethnic minority groups as a problem to be overcome, especially when factoring in religious considerations (Benn and Dagkas, 2006; Kay, 2007). An obvious way to address such issues would be to embrace the cultural differences of any given class and use this as a starting point rather than impose less relevant preferences held by the class teacher (Theodoulides, 2003). Where tensions can occur in primary Physical Education settings is around the removal of jewellery and clothing when changing. In reality most tensions that occur are rooted miscommunication and misinterpretation between parent, child and teacher, and further face-to-face conversations typically quickly resolve such matters (Griggs, 2007). Given the potential for cross-curricular planning within primary school environments, practitioners would do well to see the cultural differences contained within their classes as a resource. What may result from such a standpoint has the potential to create something more meaningful for all involved.

THOUGHT BOX

In an International school it is possible that none of the children are from the same ethnic background. Taking this standpoint and applying it to primary Physical Education, which activities should make up an appropriate curriculum?

Conclusion

Though our engagement in physical activity is patterned by gender, social class and ethnicity it is not, in theory at least, constrained by it. For example, just because there is legacy of gender appropriateness, it does not mean that when delivering primary Physical Education it should be adhered to. In fact, primary Physical Education lessons are ideal moments within which to challenge widely held assumptions pertaining to gender, social class and ethnicity. Of greater concern would be a teacher delivering primary Physical Education ignorant of the issues outlined in this chapter as the perpetuation of inappropriate stereotypes and prejudices represents another missed opportunity. It may be difficult to address the broader societal and cultural constraints within a particular setting but that does not mean that we should not try.

KEY READINGS

For those unfamiliar with the areas outlined in this chapter, one would be advised to find a well-established textbook within either Physical Education or Sports Studies and look to locate chapters on gender, social class and ethnicity. An example would be Kirk, D., Macdonald, D. and O'Sullivan, M. (eds) *The Handbook of Physical Education* (London: Sage). Useful chapters here are written by Flintoff and Scraton (Girls and Physical Education), Harrison and Belcher (Race and ethnicity in Physical Education) and Evans and Davies (Social class and Physical Education).

References

Bairner, A. (2007) Back to basics: class, social theory and sport, *Sociology of Sport Journal*, 24(1), 20–36.

Ball, S. (2009) New class inequalities in education. Why education policy is looking in the wrong place! Education policy, civil society and social class. Paper presented at the Centre for Research in social policy conference, 22–23 January, University of Loughborough, Loughborough, UK.

Benn, T. and Dagkas, S. (2006) Incompatible? Compulsory mixed-sex Physical Education Initial Teacher Training (PEITT) and the inclusion of Muslim women: A case-study on seeking solutions, *European Physical Education Review*, 12(2), 181–200.

Bourdieu, P. (1984) *Distinction: A Social Critique of the Judgement of Taste*. London: Routledge and Kegan Paul.

Bourdieu, P. (1986) The forms of capital. In J. Richardson (ed.) *Handbook of Theory and Research for the Sociology of Education*. New York: Greenwood Press.

Cahn, S. (1995) *Coming on Strong: Gender and Sexuality in Twentieth-century Women's Sport*. Cambridge, MA: Harvard University Press.

Capel, S. (2007) Moving beyond physical education subject knowledge to develop knowledgeable teachers of the subject, *Curriculum Journal*, 18(4), 493–507.

Carroll, B. (1998) The emergence and growth of examinations in Physical education. In K. Green and K. Hardman (eds) *Physical education: A reader*. Auchen: Meyer and Meyer Verlag.

Cashmore, E. (2005) *Making Sense of Sports* (4th edition). London: E&F.N. Spon.

Coakley, J. (2008) *Sport in Society* (9th Edition). Boston: McGraw-Hill Higher Education.

Coakley, J. and White, A. (1992) Making decisions: gender and sport participation among British adolescents, *Sociology of Sport Journal*, 9, 20–35.

Coalter, F. (1996) Trends in sports participation. Position paper prepared for the sports council. Institute for Leisure and Amenity management annual conference, Birmingham, UK.

Cockburn, C. and Clarke, G. (2002) 'Everybody's looking at you!': Girls negotiating the 'femininity deficit' they incur in physical education, *Women's Studies International Forum*, 25, 651–665.

Collins, M. and Kay, T. (2003) *Sport and Social Exclusion*. London: Routledge.

Connell, R. (1987) *Gender and Power*. Redwood City, CA: Stanford University Press.

Connell, R. (1995) *Masculinities*. Los Angeles, CA: University of California Press.

Dagkas, S. and Stathi, A. (2007) Exploring social and environmental factors affecting adolescents' participation in physical activity, *European Physical Education Review*, 13(3), 369–384.

Duncan, J.M., Al-Nakeeb, Y., Nevill, A. and Jones, M.V. (2004) Body image and physical activity in British secondary school children, *European Physical Education Review*, 10(3), 243–260.

Duncan, M. and Messner, M. (1998) The media image of sport and gender. In L. Wenner (ed.) *Mediasport*. London: Routledge.

Evans, J. (2004) Making a difference: education and ability in Physical Education, *European Physical Education Review*, 10(1), 95–108.

Evans, J. and Bairner, A. (2012) Physical Education and social class. In G. Stidder and S. Hayes (eds) *Equity and Inclusion in Physical Education and Sport*. London: Routledge.

Evans, J. and Davies, B. (2005) Endnote: The embodiment of consciousness. In J. Evans, B. Davies and J. Wright (eds) *Body Knowledge and Control. Studies in the Sociology of Physical Education and Health*. London: Routledge.

Evans, J. and Davies, B. (2006) Social class and Physical Education. In D. Kirk, M. O'Sullivan and D. Macdonald (eds) *Handbook of Physical Education*. London: Sage.

Evans, J. and Davies, B. (2010) Family, class and embodiment: why school physical education makes so little difference in post school participation patterns in physical activity, *International Journal of Qualitative Studies in Education*, 23(7), 765–84.

Field, J. (2003) *Social Capital*. London: Routledge.

Fitz, J., Davies, B. and Evans, J. (2006) *Educational Policy and Social Reproduction*. London: Routledge.

Fleming, S. (1991) Sport, schooling and Asian male youth culture. In G. Jarvie (ed.) *Sport, racism and ethnicity*. London: Falmer Pres.

Flintoff, A. and Scraton, S. (2001) Stepping into active leisure? Young women's perceptions of active lifestyles and their experiences of school physical education, *Sport, Education and Society*, 6, 5–21.

Flintoff, A. and Scraton, S. (2006) Girls and physical education. In D. Kirk, D. Macdonald and M. O'Sullivan (eds) *The Handbook of Physical Education*. London: Sage.

Gorard, S., Taylor, C. and Fitz, J. (2003) *Schools, Markets and Choice Policies*. London: Routledge Falmer.

Green, K. (2003) *Physical Education Teachers on Physical Education. A Sociological Study of Philosophies and Ideologies*. Chester: Chester Academic Press.

Green, K. (2008) *Understanding Physical Education*. London: Sage.

Green, K., Smith, A. and Roberts, K. (2005) Social class, young people, sport and physical education. In K. Green and K. Hardman (eds) *Physical Education: Essential Issues*. London: Sage.

Griffiths, J. and Griggs, G. (2008) 'Miss! This is way better than what we've done before': Exploring an alternative curriculum for girls' Physical Education, *PE and Sport Today*, 16(3), 26–28.

Griggs, G. and Ward, G. (2012) Physical Education in the UK: disconnections and reconnections, *Curriculum Journal*, 23(2), 207–229.

Guttmann, A. (1994) *Games and Empires*. New York. Columbia University Press.

Hargreaves, J. (1994) *Sporting Females*. London: Routledge.

Harrison, L. and Belcher, D. (2006) Race and ethnicity in physical education. In D. Kirk, D. Macdonald and M. O'Sullivan (eds) *Handbook of Physical Education*. Thousand Oaks, CA: Sage.

Holt, R. (1989) *Sport and The British – A Modern History*. Oxford: Oxford University Press

Horne, J., Tomlinson, A. and Whannel, G. (1999) *Understanding Sport*. London: E & FN Spon.

Jarvie, G. (ed.) (1991) *Sport, racism and ethnicity*. London: Falmer Press.

Kay, T. (2007) Fathering through sport, *World Leisure Journal*, 49(2), 69–82.

Kew, F. (1997) *Sport, Social Problems and Issues*. Oxford: Butterworth-Heinemann

Kirk, D. (2004) Towards a critical history of the body, identity and health. Corporeal power and school practice. In J. Evans, B. Davies and J. Wright (eds) *Body Knowledge and Control. Studies in the Sociology of Physical Education and Health*. London: Routledge.

Leaman, O. (1984) *Sit on the Sidelines and Watch the Boys Play: Sex Differentiation in Physical Education*. York: Longman/Schools Council Publications.

Linder, K. (2002) The physical activity performance relationship revisited, *Pediatric Exercise Science*, 14, 155–169.

Macdonald, D., Rodger, S., Ziviani, J., Jenkins, D., Batch, J. and Jones, J. (2004) Physical activity as a dimension of family life for lower primary school children, *Sport, Education and Society*, 9(3), 307–325.

Mangan, J.A. (1981) *Athleticism in the Victorian and Edwardian Public School*. Cambridge: Cambridge University Press.

McDonald, I. (2003) Class inequality and the body in physical education. In G. Stidder and S. Hayes (eds) *Equity and Inclusion in Physical Education and Sport*. London: Routledge.

McIntosh, P. (1979) *Fair Play: Ethics in Sport and Education*. London: Heinemann.

McIntosh, P. (1987) *Sport in Society*. London: West London Press.

Meighan, R. and Siraj-Blachford, I. (2003) *A Sociology of Educating* (4th edition). London: Continuum.

Morgan, P. and Bourke, M. (2005) An investigation of pre-service and primary school teacher perspectives of Physical Education teaching confidence and Physical Education teacher education, *ACHPER Healthy Lifestyles Journal*, 52(1), 7–13.

Morgan, P. and Bourke, M. (2008) Non-specialist teachers' confidence to teach Physical Education: the nature and influence of personal experiences in schools, *Physical Education and Sport Pedagogy*, 13(1), 1–29.

Paechter, C. (2003) Power, bodies and identity. How different forms of PE construct varying masculinities and femininities in secondary school, *Sex Education*, 3(1), 47–59.

Porter, S. (2002) *Physical activity: an exploration of the issues and attitudes of teenage girls*. London: Scott Porter Research and Marketing.

Pressland, A. and Griggs, G. (2014) The photographic representation of female athletes in the British print media during the London 2012 Olympic Games, Sport in Society, Ifirst.

Rees, C. and Miracle, A. (2000) Education and sports. In J. Coakley and E. Dunning (eds) *Handbook of Sports Studies*. London: Sage.

Rich, E. (2003) The problem with girls: liberal feminism, equal opportunities and gender inequality in Physical Education, *British Journal of Physical Education*, 34(1) 46–49.

Rich, E. (2004) Exploring teachers' biographies and perceptions of girls' participation in physical education, *European Journal of Physical Education*, 10(2), 215–240.

Roberts, K. (1996) Young people, schools, sport and government policy, *Sport, Education and Society*, 1(1), 47–57.

Roberts, K. (1999) *Leisure in Contemporary Society*. Wallingford: CABI publishing.

Roberts, K. and Brodie, D. (1992) *Inner city sport. Who plays and what are the benefits?* Culenborg: Gordano Bruno.

Royal College of Physicians, Royal College of Paediatrics and Child Care, Faculty of Public Health (2004) Storing up problems: the medical case for a slimmer nation. Report of a working party. London: Royal College of Physicians.

Sandford, R. and Rich, E. (2006) Learners and popular culture. In D. Kirk, D. Macdonald and M. O'Sullivan (eds) *The Handbook of Physical Education*. London: Sage.

Sallis, J. and Owen, N. (1999) *Physical Activity and Behavioural Medicine*. Thousand Oaks, CA: Sage.

Shilling, C. (1991) Education the body: physical capital and the production of social inequalities, *Sociology*, 25(4), 653–672.

Shilling, C. (1993) *The Body and Social Theory*. London: SAGE.

Sport Council for Wales (2002) *Adult sports participation and class membership in Wales 2000/01*. Cardiff: SCW.

Sport England (2003) *Young People and sport in England. Trends in participation 1994–2002*. London: England.

Stidder, G., Lines, G. and Keyworth, S. (2012) Investigating the gender regime in Physical Education and dance. In G. Stidder and S. Hayes (eds) *Equity and Inclusion in Physical Education* (2nd edition). London: Routledge.

Stroot, S.A. and Ko, B. (2006). Induction of beginning physical educators into the school setting. In D. Kirk, D. Macdonald and M. O'Sullivan (eds) *The Handbook of Physical Education*. London: Sage Publications.

Sugden, J. and Tomlinson, A. (2002) Theorising sport, class and status. In J. Coakley and E. Dunning (eds) *Handbook of Sports Studies*. London: Sage.

Theberge, N. (1989) Women's athletics and the myth of female frailty. In J. Freeman (ed.) *Women: A Feminist Perspective* (4th edition). Mountain View, CA: Mayfield.

Theberge, N. (2000) Gender and sport. In J. Coakley and E. Dunning (eds) *Handbook of Sports Studies*. London: Sage.

Theodoulides, A. (2003) Curriculum planning for inclusion in physical education. In Hayes, S. and Stidder, G. (eds) *Equality and Inclusion in Physical Education and Sport*. London: Routledge.

Tranter, N. (1998) *Sport, Economy and Society in Britain 1750–1914*. Cambridge: Cambridge University Press.

Vincent, C. and Ball, S. (2007) Making up the middle class child. Families, acquisition and class dispositions, *Sociology*, 41(6), 1061–1077.

Wanless, D. (2004) Securing good health for the whole population. Final report. London: Department of Health.

Wright, J. and Burrows, L. (2006) Re-concepting ability in Physical Education: a social analysis', *Sport, Education and Society*, 11(3), 275–291.

Wright, J., Macdonald, D. and Groom, L. (2003) Physical activity and young people beyond participation, *Sport, Education and Society*, 8(1), 17–33.

10

BUILDING BRIDGES

Managing transitions within Physical Education

Introduction

The educational research on transition between primary schools (for children aged 5–11 years) to secondary school (for children aged 11–16) shows that it is a period of anxiety for many children (Galton and Morrison, 2000; Jindal-Snape and Foggie, 2006), The significance of the transition from primary to secondary school in the UK and its global equivalent has been viewed as one of the most difficult in pupils' educational careers (Zeedyk et al., 2003) and a 'key rite of passage' (Pratt and George, 2005: 16). Though research shows that children entering secondary schooling look forward to having more choices and making new friends, at the same time they appear concerned about being picked on and teased by older children, having harder work, getting lower grades, and getting lost in a larger, unfamiliar school (Measor and Woods, 1984; Mizelle, 1999; Lucey and Reay, 2000). Such anxiety appears to result in a substantial decline in self-esteem, academic motivation and achievement (Eccles and Midgley, 1989; Wigfield et al., 1991; Anderson et al., 2000; Jindal-Snape and Miller, 2008).

Subjects such as Physical Education are not immune from such effects. During this period studies have reported that physical activity (PA) shows a significant rate of decline (World Health Organization, 2007) as do attitudes towards Physical Education (Lawrence, 2006). Indeed Katene (2001) suggests that Physical Education is an area of the curriculum which requires particular attention given that pupils are exposed to enormous sports halls, 'proper' gymnastics equipment, physical education specialists and structured PE lessons, in many cases for the first time. The former National Curriculum for Physical Education document advocated that focusing on such an important transition is integral to achieving high quality PE (DfEE/QCA, 1999) and failure to do so can undo much of the good work that may have been done to continue the development of a child's lifelong physical activity (Rainer and Cropley, 2013). Transition literature consistently uses the term 'bridges' as crucial links that must be negotiated as children move between primary and secondary schools (Galton et al., 1999; Parkman et al., 2005; Rainer and Cropley, 2013). Though not all agree on the same bridges or terminology, the concept is used here as a useful tool to explain significant areas that should be understood within Physical Education.

Building administrative bridges

In a culture of performativity and pupil monitoring there is more data available within primary schools than ever before (Ball, 2003). Consequently, significant amounts of data are typically passed on from primary schools to secondary schools. Research suggests that though robust mechanisms are in place regarding general pupil record transfer, with an academic focus on performance in subjects such as English and Maths, administrative practices concerning foundation subjects such as Physical Education are of a much lower priority (Dismore and Bailey, 2010). More recent findings suggest that while the vast majority of schools have a general school transition policy, few if any schools have any provision within their transition policy for Physical Education (Rainer and Cropley, 2013). The passing on of records in this area seems to vary in both quality and quantity with large numbers of primary schools failing to provide anything meaningful to their secondary counterparts. Consequently, this leads in the main to secondary staff reading the documentation but essentially ignoring its content (Lance, 1994; McCallum, 1996; Talbot, 1996; Capel et al., 2004). Indeed recent empirical research in this area serves to highlight the professional mistrust that persists between primary and secondary teachers concerning Physical Education and with the 'us and them' culture acting as a barrier to effective transition from Key Stage 2 to Key Stage 3 (Rainer and Cropley, 2013)

Addressing this issue is an obvious place to start with the need to establish better working relationships between primary and secondary staff within subject areas such as Physical Education (Parkman et al., 2005). Within this working relationship a shared understanding of assessment then needs to be built and implemented (Katene, 2001). If the assessment information passed on is therefore seen to be fair and objective, and secondary colleagues have confidence in its validity, there should be no reason for them to continue with a fresh start policy (see SEED, 1999). It is also recommended that information passed on at transfer should include more than details of academic attainment within a given area (Jindal-Snape and Miller, 2008). In Physical Education this could include 'attainment level, sporting achievement, personal circumstances, ability level, as well as the statutory end of key stage information that progresses with the pupil' (Rainer and Cropley, 2013: 1).

> **THOUGHT BOX**
>
> What practical ways could help to establish better working relationships between primary and secondary staff within subject areas such as Physical Education?

Building curriculum bridges

As indicated in Chapter 3, there remains a long-standing concern that the Physical Education curriculum remains disconnected at different points, not least between Key Stages 2 and 3 as children move from primary school to secondary school. The absence of progressive steps may prevent children moving effectively from the simple activities of the early years to the more complex activities of later childhood and beyond (NASPE, 1995; Jess et al., 2004). It is a widely held view that putting the right building blocks in place from the bottom up builds a much stronger and sustainable curriculum model and increases the chances of lifelong participation in physical activity (see Gallahue and Ozmun, 1995; Almond, 1997; Jess et al., 2004; Haydn-Davies, 2005; Griggs, 2007).

Previous studies and reports have consistently suggested that curriculum bridges should focus on improving the continuity in the curriculum between primary and secondary schools in Physical Education (Talbot, 1996; Ofsted, 2002; Zwozdiak-Myers, P. 2002; Capel et al, 2004). It therefore remains somewhat surprising that the secondary Physical Education curriculum has continued to be delivered with little appreciation of pupils' previous experience, knowledge or understanding in this area (Hepworth, 1999; Talbot, 2009; Rainer and Cropley, 2013). Evidence of what has been termed a fresh start approach (Jarman, 1990; Gorwood, 1991; SEED, 1999; Galton et al. 2003; Lance, 1994; Jindal-Snape and Miller, 2008) results in pupils dipping in their learning (Howarth and Head, 1988; Ellis, 1999; Capel et al., 2003) which is caused in the main by teachers creating a 'circular curriculum' whereby pupils repeat tasks previously covered (Jones and Jones, 1993; Lawrence, 2006). Pupil perceptions of transition within Physical Education appears to be split. On the one hand, the disconnected curriculum acts as a barrier often at the root of negative attitudes that develop towards physical education (Subramaniam and Silverman, 2002). On the other, the increased breadth of activities to which children were exposed results in a positive attitude for others (Luke and Sinclair, 1991; Carlson, 1995; Subramaniam and Silverman, 2002; Dismore and Bailey, 2010).

Building pedagogical bridges

As indicated in Chapter 5 there is a wide range of teaching styles that can be adopted when delivering Physical Education. At one end a command style approach sees information given didactically by a teacher, dominant and central to the learning environment. At the other end more child centred approaches allow for investigation and exploration where the teacher takes on more of a facilitator role (Mosston and Ashworth, 2002). Typically the different ends of the spectrum are more likely to occur in secondary and primary environments respectively (Tsangaridou, 2006; Kirk, 2010) and is explained by Benyon (1981) as secondary teachers teach subjects and primary teachers teach children. Dismore and Bailey (2010) found that different approaches to teaching were reportedly adopted by primary and secondary Physical Education teachers. Learning environments in primary schools were seen as more fun where in secondary schools they were more structured. Pupil feedback did little to counter any long-standing stereotypes in the study conducted by Rainer and Cropley (2013) where the Physical Education teacher in the secondary school was said to shout instructions all the time and intimidate and scare the pupils.

Underlying issues here resonate with earlier points made concerning an 'us and them' culture. Though children should not necessarily expect the way something is delivered in one environment to be the same as in another, as Mosston and Ashworth's (2002) spectrum indicates (see Chapter 5) there are ways to deliver that are common to all teachers and these should be in any good teacher's toolkit. Ultimately all teachers should be interested in developing the children they are responsible for to learn and it is from this point that a common dialogue should be found (Katene, 2001). The transition from primary school to secondary school could be an opportunity for those involved in the delivery of Physical Education to develop cross-phase dialogue, share teaching practice and exchange ideas which would allow those stereotypical images formed of each other by teachers to be challenged and hopefully reassessed (Rainer and Cropley, 2013).

Managing personal and social learning experiences

There is evidence that schools are frequently less concerned with personal and social concerns of children at transition than they are with easing organisational or administrative procedures (Boyd, 2005). Yet such concerns should not be overlooked as insignificant or trivial within the transition process. A significant stressor during transition seems to be that peer relationships are often in a state of flux with children who have been classmates for years suddenly becoming strangers. The nature of peer status changes too, 'as children go from being "big fish in a small pool" to minnows in an uncharted ocean. As they adjust to the new environment, the new organisational arrangements, the new relationships and the new sets of rules (both explicit and hidden), there may be conflict between social and educational agendas' (Jindal-Snape and Miller, 2008: 222). Some 30 years ago, Measor and Woods (1984) highlighted that at this time children can experience a sense of loss – loss of the familiar, in terms of places, people and routines. Despite the passage of time, this still seems true for each generation (Tonkin and Watt, 2003; Dismore and Bailey, 2010).

Beyond generic personal and social issues concerning transition the Physical Education environment is thought to provide a distinctive setting for peer socialisation (Hargreaves and Galton, 2002). The significance of the body and in particular how it looks, feels and performs can be difficult for some children particularly as part of their embryonic adolescent identity (Pellegrini and Long, 2002). Also substantive Physical Education literature suggests that secondary schools' reproduction of traditional, organised, competitive sports, creates contexts in which some are more able, suited or permitted to take part than others (Penney and Evans, 1997; Wellard, 2002; Evans, 2004). Dismore and Bailey (2010) concluded that Physical Education can act as a powerful medium for social development, especially when moving schools can heighten the processes of social inclusion/exclusion (Bailey, 2007). Given that considerable literature indicates that initiating children into physical activities will not necessarily result in positive development (Bailey et al., 2009), those who have seen Physical Education or sporting opportunities as a way of quickly socially integrating children during transition (e.g. through a festival) may be somewhat naive in their viewpoint. Indeed, Dismore and Bailey (2010: 181) indicate that 'without the mediating force of a skilled teacher who is able to present these activities within a certain form of value system, it may well be the case that physical education exaggerates, rather than challenges alienation, exclusion and disengagement from physical activities'.

Finding clear, detailed recommendations for effective transitions between primary and secondary should be straightforward but close inspection of many appear generic and cannot be applied either to the bridges concept outlined in the chapter or to individual subject areas such as Physical Education. Some of the clearest and most helpful recommendations informed by academic and action-research findings on what works in improving transition of pupils between primary and secondary schools are those published by Parkman et al. (2005). Here five transition bridges have been identified, as opposed to the four outlined in the chapter. In effect, the 'Managing personal and social learning experiences' subheading used in the chapter has been split by Parkman et al. (2005) to form a fifth bridge. Though the language is not specifically for Physical Education transition, there are enough detailed points from which to work and apply the recommendations for an individual subject area (see Box 10.1).

Conclusion

Making transitions between schools is a difficult time for children, parents and teachers. It is a time where familiar places to people and routines have suddenly changed and all involved have a role to play to ensure that the process can occur as effectively as possible. Effective transition has the best chance of occurring if a focus remains on the child, principally their self-esteem, confidence and learning. Decisions made by teachers that prioritise different agendas such as maintaining professional mistrust, do so to the detriment of each cohort of children that

BOX 10.1 TRANSITION BRIDGES AND RECOMMENDATIONS

Administrative

1. Transition policy is in place and has been agreed in partnership with primary schools. It covers the process for collecting and transferring information and sets an expectation for active work with partner school(s). It outlines the role of staff, parents and pupils in the transition process. The policy is regularly reviewed and amended accordingly. All staff, parents and pupils are aware of the policy.
2. Transition processes are broadened to include pupils in year groups other than Y7.
3. Regular meetings and good working relations between primary and secondary school staff, including: senior staff; heads of year; subject heads; SENCOs, and subject teachers.
4. Clear roles and responsibilities within primary and secondary schools that span transition. Job descriptions make these explicit.
5. A 'transition champion' is identified within the school and the Board of Governors, i.e. named individuals with responsibility for effective transition.
6. Feedback provided to primary schools on effectiveness of transition arrangements and early progress of pupils.
7. Ongoing feedback to primary schools to include Key Stage 3, GCSE and post-16 attainment.
8. Quality information provided to parents on administrative arrangements.
9. Non-teaching staff are fully involved in the transition process, e.g. support staff from primary schools work with known pupils during first few days in secondary school.
10. Staff, parents and pupils are involved in evaluating transition arrangements to secure continuous improvement.
11. Administrative arrangements for transition are tailored to the needs of specific groups of pupils, e.g. those with special educational needs, G&T, pupils with EAL.

Curriculum

1. Making effective use of common data transfer form to capture pupil level information.
2. Ensuring effective and full use of individual pupil data received from primary schools, including Key Stage 2 results and CATS.
3. Data is used effectively at whole-school, department and classroom levels.
4. Effective pupil-tracking (cohort and individual pupil) to monitor progress.
5. Setting of attainment targets and procedures to monitor progress towards these targets.
6. Cross-phase teaching, i.e. common curriculum topics that span Y6 and Y7.

7. Secondary schools receive and build on 'curriculum maps' for Key Stage 2 from feeder primary schools and adapt Y7 curriculum accordingly.
8. Two-way dialogue and discussion between primary and secondary schools on Y6 and Y7 curricula.
9. Teachers in each phase have detailed knowledge of respective assessment, tracking and target-setting processes.
10. Common understanding of progress expected of pupils during transition years.
11. Shared understanding on the quality of work expected from Y6 and Y7 pupils across at least core subjects.
12. Joint projects and cross-phase activities. Other joint provision may also include bridging units.
13. Summer schools.
14. Joint masterclasses for gifted and talented pupils.
15. Joint teacher training days and professional development.
16. Catch-up programmes in Y7, especially for literacy.
17. Quality information to parents about the curriculum. This shows what will be taught and how continuity with primary school curriculum is ensured.
18. Curriculum arrangements for transition are tailored to the needs of specific groups of pupils, e.g. those with special educational needs, G&T, pupils with EAL.

Pedagogic

1. An understanding of primary and secondary schools' approach to learning and teaching.
2. Policies on learning and teaching shared across phases.
3. A common language for discussing learning and teaching, e.g. use of terms such as 'learning objectives', 'plenary', 'response partner' etc.
4. Teacher exchange and secondment between primary and secondary schools.
5. Shared lesson observations.
6. Team teaching.
7. Advanced Skills Teachers provide outreach support to primary schools.
8. Joint training programmes and professional development on teaching skills.
9. Recognition and celebration of differences in learning and teaching, e.g. access to specialist teaching and resources.
10. Groupings of students in Y7 which reduce the impact of change, e.g. same teacher for English, humanities and citizenship.
11. Active preparation of pupils to meet new ways of working.
12. Quality information to parents about teaching and classroom practice.

13. Common approach to learning environments, e.g. accessibility of resources, use of display to promote learning, arrangement of classroom furniture, etc.
14. Schools in both phases evaluate and adapt their joint approach to transition – taking account of the views of pupils, teachers and parents.
15. Pedagogy is tailored to the needs of specific groups of pupils, e.g. those with special educational needs, G&T, pupils with EAL.

Social and personal

1. Induction days with clear purpose and outcome.
2. Open evenings for pupils and parents.
3. Specialist visits are held across the full range of curriculum subjects, e.g. ICT, drama, sports, science.
4. Parent and pupil guides for new entrants.
5. Enabling pupils to access their new learning environment with confidence – using year/home bases as appropriate.
6. Parents and pupils are effectively 'briefed' about transition, with opportunities to feed back on the reality for them.
7. Joint social events between current Y6 and Y7 pupils.
8. Identifying, in partnership with primary schools, and responding to pupils with particular difficulties, needs or strengths.
9. Using information on social groupings within primary schools to create class groups.
10. Pupil peer mentoring – pre- and post-transition – and social support.
11. Sharing of information from primary school on social groupings.
12. Quality information to parents about pastoral support and differences in the school.
13. Parents have an early opportunity to discuss progress and transition issues with secondary school staff.
14. Robust anti-bullying policy that is made explicit to pupils and parents and implemented effectively.
15. Social, personal and pastoral arrangements for transition are tailored to the needs of specific groups of pupils, e.g. those with special educational needs, G&T, pupils with EAL.

Autonomy and managing learning

1. Pupils (and teachers) understand their preferred learning styles and can talk confidently about this to their new teachers (and pupils).
2. Similar language is used across phases to talk about learning and teaching.
3. Pupils develop a learning portfolio which describes them as learners and

gives samples of achievements. This is shared with the secondary school and extended during Y7.

4. Pupils are actively encouraged to become 'professional learners' – reflecting on what and how they are learning.
5. Pupils are empowered to proactively contribute to the transition process and are viewed as active participants, e.g. suggesting improvements and identifying barriers to successful transition.
6. Quality information is given to parents about their contribution to managing learning and encouraging their children to become 'professional learners'.
7. Learning is managed to meet the needs of specific groups of pupils, e.g. those with special educational needs, G&T, pupils with EAL.

(Adapted from Parkman et al., 2005)

they teach. Research shows however that some of the problems here are long standing and deep rooted, and need careful thought about how best to move forwards more effectively. The recommendations shown here are useful starting points in this process and while perhaps not all the recommendations listed here would be adopted in a given environment, some pertinent ones could easily be adopted to ease transition, while others are worked towards. The separation of these ideas into different transition bridges should also help professionals think about the different ways in which their practice impacts upon the transition process.

KEY READINGS

There is a dearth of research in this area but there are, to date, arguably three key papers that examine the transition from primary school to secondary school pertaining to Physical Education. These are first, Capel, S., P. Zwozdiak-Myers and Lawrence, J. (2004) Exchange of information about Physical Education to support the transition of pupils from primary and secondary school, *Educational Research*, 46(3), 283–300. Second, Dismore, H. and Bailey, R. (2010) 'It's been a bit of a rocky start': attitudes towards Physical Education following transition, *Physical Education and Sport Pedagogy*, 15(2), 175–191. And last, but most recent, Rainer, P. and Cropley, B. (2013) Bridging the gap – but mind you don't fall. Primary Physical Education teachers' perceptions of the transition process to secondary school, *Education 3–13*, doi: 10.1080/03004279.2013.819026.

References

Almond, L. (1997) *Physical Education in Schools* (2nd edition). London: Kogan Page.

Anderson, L., Jacobs, J., Schramm, F. and Splittgerber, S. (2000) School transitions: beginning of the end or new beginning?, *International Journal of Educational Research*, 33(4), 325–339.

Bailey, R.P. (2007) Youth sport and social inclusion. In N. Holt (ed.) *Positive Youth Development Through Sport*. London: Routledge.

Bailey, R.P., Armour, K., Kirk, D., Jess, M., Pickup, I. and Sandford, R. (2009) The educational benefits claimed for physical education and school sport: an academic review, *Research Papers in Education*, 24(1), 1–27.

Ball, S.J. (2003) The teacher's soul and the terrors of performativity, *Journal of Education Policy*, 18(2), 215–228.

Benyon, L. (1981) Curriculum continuity, *Education*, 9(1), 3–13.

Boyd, B. (2005) *Primary/Secondary Transition: An Introduction to the Issues*. Paisley: Hodder.

Capel, S., Zwozdiak-Myers, P. and Lawrence, J. (2003) A study of current practice in liaison between primary and secondary schools in physical education, *European Physical Education Review*, 9(2), 115–135.

Capel, S., Zwozdiak-Myers, P. and Lawrence, J. (2004) Exchange of information about Physical Education to support the transition of pupils from primary and secondary school, *Educational Research*, 46(3), 283–300.

Carlson, T. (1995) 'We hate gym': student alienation from physical education, *Journal of Teaching in Physical Education*, 14(4), 467–471.

Department for Education and Employment/Qualifications and Curriculum Authority (DfEE/QCA) (1999) *The National Curriculum in England and Wales; Physical Education*. London: HMSO.

Dismore, H. and Bailey, R. (2010) 'It's been a bit of a rocky start': attitudes towards Physical Education following transition, *Physical Education and Sport Pedagogy*, 15(2), 175–191.

Eccles, J.S. and Midgley, C. (1989). Stage-environment fit: developmentally appropriate classrooms for young adolescents. In C. Ames and R. Ames (eds) *Research on Motivation in Education: Goals and Cognitions, Volume 3*. New York: Academic.

Ellis, S. (1999) National Curriculum testing across the interface at KS2/KS3: a view from the bridge, *Curriculum*, 20(1), 38–51.

Evans, J. (2004) Making a difference? Education and 'ability' in Physical Education, *European Physical Education Review*, 10(1), 95–106.

Gallahue, D. and Ozmun, J. (1995) *Understanding Motor Development: Infants, Children, Adolescents, Adults* (3rd edition). Madison, WI: Brown and Benchmark.

Galton, M. and Morrison, I. (2000) Concluding comments: Transfer and transition: the next steps, *International Journal of Educational Research*, 33, 443–449.

Galton, M., Gray, J. and Ruddock, J. (2003) *Transfer and Transitions in the Middle Years of Schooling (7–14): Continuities and Discontinuities in Learning*. London: HMSO.

Galton, M., Hargreaves, M., Comber, C., Wall, D. and Pell, A. (1999) *Inside the Primary Classroom: 20 Years On*. London: Routledge.

Gorwood, B. (1991) Primary-secondary transfer after the National Curriculum, *School Organisation*, 11(3), 283–290.

Griggs, G. (2007) Physical Education: primary matters, secondary importance, *Education 3–13*, 35(1), 59–69.

Hargreaves, L. and Galton, M. (2002) *Transfer From the Primary Classroom 20 Years On*. London: Routledge Falmer.

Haydn-Davies, D. (2005) How does the concept of physical literacy relate to what is and what could be the practice of Physical Education? *British Journal of Teaching Physical Education*, 36(3), 45–48.

Hepworth, N. (1999) Continuity and Progression: Key Stages 2 and 3, *Bulletin of Physical Education*, 35(1), 23–35.

Howarth, K. and Head, R. (1988) Curriculum continuity in physical education: a small scale study, *British Journal of Physical Education*, 19(6), 241–243.

Jarman, R. (1990) Primary–secondary science continuity: a new ERA?, *School Science Review*, 71(257), 19–29.

Jess, M., Dewar, K. and Fraser, G. (2004). Basic moves: developing a foundation for lifelong physical activity, *British Journal of Teaching in Physical Education*, 35(2), 23–27.

Jindal-Snape, D. and Foggie, J. (2006) Moving stories: A research study exploring children/ young people, parents and practitioners' perceptions of primary–secondary transitions. Report for Transitions Partnership Project, University of Dundee, Dundee.

Jindal-Snape, D. and Miller, D. (2008) A challenge of living? Understanding the psycho-social processes of the child during primary–secondary transition through resilience and self-esteem theories, *Educational Psychology Review*, 20(3), 217–236.

Jones, L.P. and Jones, L. (1993) Keeping up the momentum: improving continuity, *Education 3–13*, 21(3), 46–50.

Katene, W. (2001) Progression and continuity in Physical Education between primary and secondary school. In S. Capel and S. Piotrowski (eds) *Issues in Physical Education*. London: Routledge.

Kirk, D. (2010) *Physical Education Futures*. London: Routledge.

Lance, A. (1994) The Case for Continuity, *Forum*, 36(2), 46–47.

Lawrence, J. (2006) Negotiating change: The impact of school transfer on attainment, self-esteem, self motivation and attitudes in physical education. PhD diss., Brunel University, Bristol.

Lucey, H., and Reay, D. (2000) Identities in transition: anxiety and excitement in the move to secondary school, *Oxford Review of Education*, 26,191–205.

Luke, M. and Sinclair, G. (1991) Gender differences in adolescents' attitudes toward school physical education, *Journal of Teaching in Physical Education*, 11(1), 31–46.

McCallum, B. (1996) The Transfer and Use of Assessment Between Primary and Secondary Schools, *British Journal of Curriculum and Assessment*, 16(3), 10–14.

Measor, L. and Woods, P. (1984) *Changing Schools: Pupil Perspectives on Transfer to a Comprehensive*. Buckingham: Open University Press.

Mizelle, N.B. (1999) Helping middle school students make the transition into high school. ERIC Digest. ED432411. Available online at http://ericir.syr.edu/plweb-cgi/ obtain.pl (accessed 2 August 2002).

Mosston, M. and Ashworth, S. (2002) *Teaching Physical Education* (5th edition). London: Pearson Education.

National Association for Physical Education (NASPE) (1995) *Moving Into the Future: National Physical Education Standards: A Guide to Content and Assessment*. St Louis, MI: Mosby.

Office for Standards in Education (OFSTED) (2002) *Changing Schools: An Evaluation of the Effectiveness of Transfer Arrangements at Age 11 (HMI 550)*. London: HMSO.

Parkman, M., Fuller, K. and Horswell, C. (2005) *Key Stage 2 to Key Stage 3 Transition Project*. London: Department for Education and Skills.

Pellegrini, A. and Long, J. (2002) A longitudinal study of bullying, dominance and victimisation during the transition from primary school through secondary school, *British Journal of Developmental Psychology*, 20(2), 259–280.

Penney, D. and Evans, J. (1997) Naming the game: discourse and domination in physical education and sport in England and Wales, *European Physical Education Review*, 3(1), 21–32.

Pratt, S. and George, R. (2005) Transferring friendship: girls' and boys' friendship in the transition from primary to secondary school, *Children and Society*, 19(1), 16–26.

Rainer, P. and Cropley, B. (2013) Bridging the gap – but mind you don't fall. Primary physical education teachers' perceptions of the transition process to secondary school, *Education 3–13*, doi: 10.1080/03004279.2013.819026.

SEED (1999) *Review of Assessment in Pre-school and 5–14*. Edinburgh: HMSO.

Subramaniam, P. and Silverman, S. (2002) Using complimentary data: an investigation of student attitudes in physical education, *Journal of Sport Pedagogy*, 8(1), 74–91.

Talbot, M. (1996) Gender and national curriculum physical education, *British Journal of Physical Education*, 27(1), 5–7.

Talbot, M. (2009) The Rose Primary Review: a case study in influence and advocacy, *Physical Education Matters*, 3(2), 6–10.

Tonkin, S.E. and Watt, H.M.G. (2003) Self-concept over the transition from primary to secondary school: a case study on a program for girls, *Issues in Educational Research*, 13(2), 27–54.

Tsangaridou, N. (2006) Teachers' beliefs. In D. Kirk, D. Macdonald and M. O'Sullivan (eds) *The Handbook of Physical Education*. London: Sage.

Wellard, I. (2002) Men, sport, body performance and the maintenance of exclusive masculinity, *Leisure Studies*, 21(3) 235–247.

Wigfield, A., Eccles, J.S., MacIver, D., Redman, D. A. and Midgley, C. (1991) Transitions during early adolescence: changes in children's domain-specific self-perceptions and general self-esteem across the transition to junior high school, *Developmental Psychology*, 27, 552–565.

World Health Organisation (2007) Inequalities in Young People's Health: HBSC International Report from the 2005/2006 Survey. Available online at www.euro.who.int/.../health...health/.../inequalities-in-young-peoples-health/ (accessed October 2012).

Zeedyk, S., Gallacher, J., Henderson, M., Hope, G., Husband, G. and Lindsay, K. (2003) Negotiating the transition from primary to secondary school: perceptions of pupils, parents and teachers, *School Psychology International*, 24(1), 67–79.

Zwozdiak-Myers, P. (2002) Exemplars of 'good practice' – in the transfer of pupils from Key Stage 2 to Key Stage 3 in Physical Education, *British Journal of Physical Education*, 33(3), 39–41.

11

WHAT DOES THE FUTURE HOLD FOR PRIMARY PHYSICAL EDUCATION?

Introduction

What becomes clear from reading this text is that understanding primary Physical Education is a complex world of interrelationships. While it might be argued that because of such complexity its future would be difficult to predict, it is precisely because of this complexity that reasonable speculations can be made. Both Jess et al. (2011) and Griggs (2012) have drawn on ideas of complexity theory to make sense of the evolutions that have occurred within primary Physical Education. Largely pioneered in the field of economics (Arthur, 1989, 1990; Holland, 1987) complexity theory is 'a theory of change, evolution, adaptation and development for survival. It breaks with simple successionist cause-and-effect models ... and a reductionist approach to understanding phenomena' (Morrison, 2008: 19) – an approach increasingly advocated by social science scholars to better engage with the micro-dynamics which underlie social processes (Jacobson, 2000; Puddifoot, 2000). When systems or institutions like schools are complex, what must be studied are the interrelationship, interaction and interconnectivity of elements or actors within a system, and between that system and its context (Chan, 2001; Santonus, 1998; Wheatley, 1999; Youngblood, 1997). Most importantly, as Davies (2004: 19) explains, complexity theory 'is not a grand narrative in terms of an overarching explanatory theory of behaviour, but more of a way of seeing connections and possibilities'. Useful tools within complex systems can be identified and considered to make sense of them. These include non-linearity, initial conditions and amplification, self-organisation, attractors, information and the edge of chaos (see Davies, 2004, for a full explanation). The problem however is that these useful tools can only be used effectively after the event, examining historical trends and patterns. But what if we could create future histories? The artefacts would allow us to explore the complexity of the events that occurred and see how they unfolded. By the use of ethnographic fiction this chapter aims to do just that.

Using fiction writing to explore ideas in primary Physical Education

The use of fictional writing techniques within academic study remains unusual but within the last decade it has become a more common practice within the fields of both sport and education (see Jones, 2007; Nelson and Groom, 2012; Roberts, 2014; Selbie and Clough, 2005). Typically the author creates fictional extracts of text which are often composites of thoughts, conversations and events to capture the essence of a particular issue (Sparkes, 2002). What they allow the reader to do is reflect upon the text and relate to the landscape. This helps the reader to consider their standpoint and helps to raise pertinent questions and issues (Ely et al., 1997). Below, five scenarios of what might be the future of primary Physical Education have been written. They are all fictional and have been set in 2040, some 25 years into the future. After reading them the intention is to consider them as historical artefacts (as if read after 2040) and using ideas within complexity theory, explain the resultant landscape.

Scenario A

From 2015 to 2040 primary Physical Education has become increasingly focused on a renewed interest in exactly what is required to deliver high quality developmental Physical Education. The catalyst for this sea change can be traced back to 2018. Up until this point outsourcing of extra-curricular sport and curriculum Physical Education had grown exponentially since the workload reform policy of 2005. Against a backdrop of less-than-confident teachers who had been given little training, the use of outsourcing was further fuelled by the pupil premium introduced following the London 2012 Olympics. When external companies saw that £9,000 had been allocated to each primary school to develop Physical Education and school sport they indiscriminately touted themselves around the primary schools in their areas, promising to deliver all or any extra-curricular sport and curriculum Physical Education sessions on offer. In 2018 a local rugby club had done just that and had been permitted by a primary school to deliver all aspects of their on-site curricular Physical Education programme including games, dance, gymnastics, athletics and Outdoor and Adventurous Activities. In the autumn of that year, during a gymnastics lesson a tragic accident occurred in which a Year 5 pupil landed awkwardly and died shortly afterwards. The enquiry that followed attracted considerable media scrutiny. The key questions that dominated the press for days afterwards were: Why were we letting rugby coaches into schools to teach gymnastics? Why weren't we training teachers properly to deliver Physical Education? Why were primary schools putting their pupils at risk on a daily basis? A major tabloid ran the headline 'The true cost of Olympic Legacy'.

The enquiry could not legally apportion blame to any individual or organisation as medical reports found that the pupil who died had a spinal defect that had not been previously known. The report indicated that the impact from the fall had jolted the spine at an awkward angle and that the resulting complications from the injury were the most likely cause of death rather than due to negligence. However the report did also indicate that the individuals leading the sessions were 'in all good common sense less than suitable', and recommended that more and better quality primary Physical Education teacher training be statutory. In Parliament the opposition Member of Parliament who represented the constituency in which the accident occurred led the campaign in the House of Commons and the opposition leader pushed the Prime Minister on the issue during Prime Minister's question time. The resulting adjustment to legislation saw statutory minimums introduced for 'higher risk' areas of the national curriculum, which included Physical Education. Inspection reports of primary Physical Education lessons were mixed at first but as better trained teachers entered the profession, standards began to rise again. Within a decade and a half research indicated that secondary schools were noticing many more similarities in abilities from their feeder primary schools rather than the wide variety they had experienced beforehand.

External agencies were prohibited from delivering curricular sessions in all areas unless delivering individuals were themselves suitably qualified teachers and were approved by the local authority. The enquiry highlighted that in some primary schools long-standing arrangements had seen secondary Physical Education staff delivering and supporting primary Physical Education lessons. Though secondary schools met the new criteria for delivery that was deemed safe, secondary staff became required to engage on subject specific CPD that trained them on developing activities that were appropriate for the pupils taking part. The accident highlighted that the gymnastic activity provided in the lesson 'did not pay due consideration either to the age or ability of the pupils'. The report recommended that anyone delivering lessons in a school 'should have sufficient knowledge to develop lessons according to the age or ability of the pupil'.

Though the practice was not widely adopted, some schools employed or shared a specialist primary Physical Education teacher. These were not part of the external agency community previously employed in schools but largely drawn from new recruits who had completed their primary teacher training with an additional primary Physical Education course. For a brief time after the accident, schools were reluctant to engage in any kind of relationship with external agencies. However over time local authority approved individuals and organisations re-established their delivery of extra-curricular school provision.

Scenario B

From 2015 to 2035 Physical Education became an increasing problem area for primary schools. Consequently in 2035, the latest curriculum review removed it altogether from the primary national curriculum. Research at the end of the twentieth century and at the start of the twenty-first century had indicated the lack of training given to teachers resulting in a lack of competence, confidence and general willingness to deliver curricular Physical Education. In the short term some of the problems were alleviated by outsourcing the lessons to external agencies, such as sports coaches. This developed further in 2025 when workload reform policies allowed primary teachers to take one day per week to help complete planning, preparation and assessment. The growing inevitable truth began to be realised that no one actually wanted primary Physical Education. For headteachers the cost benefits were beneficial, as specialist spaces and provision were no longer needed. Primary teachers who had long struggled with the apparent demands of the subject no longer had to worry about its delivery. The catalyst for the change was provoked by a string of government Education Secretaries who became increasingly preoccupied by the country's falling position in global educational league tables. The neo-liberalist agenda that had continued to dominate politics had become so obsessed with the apparent 'quiet long-term decline of young people's educational attainment' that more hours needed to be found for key skills for the twenty-first and twenty-second centuries and further improvements in Maths and English. Questions had been repeatedly raised during endless curriculum reviews about the use of certain subjects. Objections had been made by educational groups preaching the need for 'breadth' and a 'love of learning' and by subject associations, including Physical Education. All objections fell on deaf ears as the government dominated both decision making and the media narrative.

Schools were still required to facilitate sporting opportunities, not unlike the public school model established in the nineteenth century. These were delivered by a mixture of external agencies and some willing teaching staff. Commonly sports were offered on some afternoons, within an ever-lengthening school day. An emerging trend has seen greater funding for specific sports through National Governing Bodies. Team sports once again have been given the lion's share and yet again this has been justified in the country's pursuit of greater sporting success and medals. How is it no one gets the fact that netball and rugby are still not Olympic sports and the last time we entered a football team in the Olympics was 28 years ago during the London 2012 Games?

The newly created Association for Physical Activity and School Sport (AfPaSS) begins a mission to engage schools in delivering high quality Physical Activity and School Sport. Critical papers written by established academics appear in related journals asking searching questions in their titles such as 'Where did it all go wrong?' and 'Physical Education: dead or dormant?' Leading health organisations have also joined the debate since the new curriculum document was written five years ago. Preliminary research raises concerns that removing

Physical Education has resulted in young people 'doing even less overall physical activity than they did before'. Findings show that 'some young people appear to have dropped out of physical activity before the age of seven'. However these findings sit at odds with the 2040 nationally funded survey which actually shows that since the removal of Physical Education from the curriculum, children appear to be engaging in more physical activity.

Scenario C

Since the end of the twentieth century the then reported 'obesity crisis' highlighted health concerns within the wider population. Alarming figures showed how increasing numbers of children under the age of eleven were either overweight or obese. While these figures were dismissed by many, the recent increased pressure on the health service budget has led to public debates about the rising cost of sedentary behaviour. Graphic and sustained media campaigns showing morbidly obese children with provocative headlines asking 'Isn't this child abuse?' heighten public awareness. Consequently a gathering storm prior to the general election of 2038 saw all the major parties campaign on health reform and embedding a health agenda into many more aspects of society. A key plan of the now government is to promote healthy habits through schools which includes nutrition, mental well being and physical well being. Newly proposed curricular reforms have suggested a more holistic approach to primary education, locating physical aspects of the curriculum (formerly within Physical Education) within an area of Health and Well Being. It has long been known that children had been largely disaffected by Physical Education and so the draft guidelines place more of a focus on Physical Activity.

Within education these proposals have had a mixed reaction with many educationalists welcoming the shift in 'putting the child first'. Subject associations across the board, including Physical Education, have voiced their concerns, fearing the worst for their professional identity and that of its members. Seeking to remain ahead of the curve, universities have already begun to offer primary teacher training places with Health and Well Being specialisms. Outlines suggest these comprise aspects that used to be found in Physical Education, Science, Technology, Citizenship and PSHE. Recent academic papers on these proposals suggest that it will be a new breed of health professionals that might be best suited to these positions.

External agencies have begun to approach schools to develop the health of the school. Though many organisations have launched these initiatives, in this region the most popular by far is the 'Healthy Body, Healthy Mind, Healthy Future' initiative. This nationally funded project has been measuring and weighing school children and teaches cooking and fitness lessons in schools. Early results show that the pupils within the pilot schools are healthier as a result of the project.

Scenario D

Accountability based on close monitoring, recording and reporting has transformed the landscape of primary schools in 2040. Children are routinely taught and tested in core subjects such as Maths and English during each half term of their schooling. The catalyst for the change was provoked by a string of government Education Secretaries who became increasingly preoccupied by the country's falling position in global educational league tables. The neo-liberalist agenda that has continued to dominate politics has become so obsessed with the apparent 'quiet long-term decline of primary schooling'. With more apparent success achieved in secondary schooling, especially in the public school system, the new Department of Education, Employment and Training (DEET) plans of 2035 took an unforeseen turn directing all levels of education to take a subject-led approach. Primary schools have quickly begun to resemble secondary schools in recent years where staff have been appointed to deliver a single subject (or a pair in some cases) to all classes in the school.

Advocates of this approach suggest that in subjects like Physical Education this move is not before time. Research at the end of the twentieth century and at the start of the twenty-first century had indicated the lack of training given to teachers resulting in a lack of competence, confidence and general willingness to deliver curricular Physical Education. Those appointed to the roles appear to be from a mixed background. Some are drawn from new recruits who had completed their primary teacher training with an additional primary Physical Education course. Others have come from sports coaching backgrounds and some are former secondary school Physical Education teachers. Early inspection reports reveal a mixed picture with concerns raised that lessons are dominated by games and by skills development. A recent journal article has noted that 'now we have achieved the specialist teaching of primary Physical Education in schools for which we have so long campaigned, ironically what we have in practice is more reminiscent of sport than ever before'.

Scenario E

I have just given what can only be described as a depressing invited conference presentation on primary Physical Education. As 2040 represents my official retirement from the university day job I thought I'd summarise, for those who were interested, the literature that has been in circulation concerning primary Physical Education during my career. No one was surprised by issues concerning the lack of training of teachers, the low confidence and the lack of CPD. No one was surprised how sports coaches have become the norm in many schools as the chief deliverers of the subject. In fact, few were surprised at any of it apart from one still keen, fresh-faced academic. At the end of the presentation his was the first hand up to ask me a simple question: 'So what you have basically said is that, essentially, nothing has changed for 50 years. How is that possible?'

After a deep breath and an awkward smile, I replied: 'Because no one cares enough.' Buoyed by my succinct but provocative statement (and perhaps because someone still showed some interest in what I had to say), I went on to explain more fully.

'If you go back to the start of the twenty-first century we did away with subject specialists in school when we brought in new teaching standards called Qualifying to Teach. We did away with advisors and anyone, to be honest, who knew anything about primary Physical Education. Unsupported generalist teachers with little or no Physical Education training entered the profession and unsurprisingly floundered. Since then we've limped along in the same vein paying lip service to high quality primary Physical Education. We've had PESSCL, PESSYP, pupil premiums, PEPAYS and other acronyms I've forgotten about. All that ever happens is more pseudo-sport gets delivered and participation figures get measured.' After what probably sounded more like a rant than an answer, I paused, smiled and said, 'Does that answer your question?"'

He smiled back and said, 'Yes.'

Other questions were then asked to other presenters in the room, who had presented before me. The chair asked the audience if there were any final questions. Another young academic (I'm sure they get younger) put her hand up and addressed me.

She said, 'You said in your presentation that where we have got to hasn't surprised you at all. I just wondered in all the years that you have been involved in primary Physical Education, what has surprised you the most?'

'That question,' I said lamely.

After a pause, I said, 'I'm not sure it's surprise necessarily, but the one thing that I have never understood which therefore I've always found surprising is this. In all the initiatives that have ever been launched in primary schools concerning Maths and English, teachers have a clear focus for their lesson. This is communicated clearly and the teacher follows this with some form of direct teaching. Following this the class splits into different groups, depending on their ability and recent assessments. In most cases these groups are supported by different adults connected with the school. The work is done, shared and summarised, and key teaching points are reinforced. Often follow-up activities are provided and either during or after the session assessments are completed for evidence purposes and to inform planning for future lesson. These practices in one form or another have dominated classroom practice for the entirety of the twenty-first century. What I find surprising is that the same teachers walk from their classrooms to the school hall, the playground or the field and don't replicate any of those things. It's like it falls out of their head on the way. That, to this day, surprises me the most.'

The chair thanked me and all the other speakers for our presentations and, more importantly perhaps, told us where the coffee and biscuits were being served.

Some complex reflections viewed after 2040

Davies (2004) suggests that often in complex systems the evolution of events are non-linear, meaning that they do not gradually evolve in a straight line along a continuum. Typically events do evolve gradually within schooling but examination of the facts usually sees a journey sprinkled with random events which from time to time causes the predictable path to lurch off wildly in another direction. Examples of such events can be seen in Scenario A with the tragic accident, the graphic and sustained media campaign in Scenario C and the radical change in government policy in Scenario D. What this tells us is that the future cannot be predicted with any certainty within complex systems.

That said, what we can do according to Davies (2004) is look for specific aspects within a landscape and map what are termed ideal conditions and show how these can be amplified to lead on to the next event. An example across the scenarios is the lack of training given to teachers resulting in a lack of competence, confidence and general willingness to deliver curricular Physical Education. Left unchecked this issue could be so large that others will seek to check this dynamic. In Scenario A sports coaches filled the void, in Scenario C and D other health professionals and differently qualified teachers took on the role. In Scenario B events evolved that the subject was removed from the curriculum altogether. Scenario E explains briefly the creation of the ideal conditions that later became amplified.

The third idea suggested by Davies (2004) to examine complex systems was that of self-organisation. Illustrative of this idea are the sports agencies referred to in Scenario A and the health agencies referred to in Scenario C. Typically external agencies seeking to gain access to money and opportunities in another organisation are indiscriminately drawn to it at first. Multiple tenders and leafleting of schools by dozens of organisations often occur. In the long term only a few agencies survive and sustain a relationship with the established organisation. They do so by repeat work, recommendation and gaining required documentation and qualification. Thus the external agencies self-organise.

The significance of powerful attractors, acting not unlike magnets, is vital to understanding the occurrence of particular events (Davies, 2004). As explained earlier in this book, historically Physical Education sits within a nexus of Sport, Health and Education. Any increase or decrease in the power of one of these powerful attractors can see Physical Education shift its course. While it's clear that, in some scenarios (such as Scenario C), one of the three attractors dominates the other two, in others it's the interplay between the attractors that is of interest.

The last of Davies' (2004) ideas is viewing how information takes organisations to the edge of chaos creating a change in behaviour. Lewin (1993: 51) explains that 'the edge of chaos is where information gets its foot in the door'. In Scenario A, for example, the information concerned here is that 'sport' is the same as 'Physical Education' and that this information can be (and is most effectively) delivered by sports coaches. Such a situation occurs when 'there is sufficient information to create doubt ...' (Davies, 2004: 30).

THOUGHT BOX

After reading this book, which scenario do you think is more likely to occur? Do you foresee an alternative future and how will it differ from what has been presented here?

Conclusion

Though it is impossible to predict the future because real life events are complex, the extracts of ethnographic fiction used in this chapter demonstrate that possible directions of travel can be explored. Only history will show if any of them turn out to be fully accurate or accurate in part, but it is hoped that by reading this book it is possible to understand the wider socio-cultural landscape within which primary Physical Education *is, has been* and *will be* located.

KEY READINGS

For greater understanding of complexity theory in educational settings, see Davies, L. (2004) *Education and Conflict: Complexity and chaos* (London: Routledge Falmer). To understand how this has been applied to primary Physical Education contexts, see both Jess, M., Atencio, M., and Thorburn, M. (2011) Complexity Theory: supporting curriculum and pedagogy developments in Scottish Physical Education, *Sport, Education and Society* and Griggs, G. (2012) Standing on the touchline of chaos. Explaining the development of sports coaching in primary schools with the aid of complexity theory, *Education 3–13, iFirst, 259–269.* For further viewpoints on what the future might hold for Physical Education, see Kirk, D. 2010. *Physical Education Futures* (London: Routledge) and Green, K. (2012). Mission impossible? Reflecting upon the relationship between physical education, youth sport and lifelong participation, *Sport, Education and Society* (ahead of print), 1–19.

References

Arthur, W.B. (1989) Competing technologies, increasing returns, and lock-in by historical events, *The Economic Journal*, 99, 106–131.

Arthur, W.B. (1990) Positive feedbacks in the economy, *Scientific American*, 262, 92–99.

Chan, S. (2001). Complex Adaptive Systems. Paper presented at the Research Seminar in Engineering Systems, 31 October to 6 November. Massachusetts Institute of Technology Cambridge, MA.

Davies, L. (2004) *Education and Conflict: Complexity and Chaos.* London: Routledge Falmer.

Ely, M., Vinz, R., Downing, M. and Anzul, M. (1997) *On Writing Qualitative Research: Living by Words.* London: Falmer.

Green, K. (2012) Mission impossible? Reflecting upon the relationship between physical education, youth sport and lifelong participation, *Sport, Education and Society* (ahead of print), 1–19.

Griggs, G. (2012) Standing on the touchline of chaos. Explaining the development of sports coaching in primary schools with the aid of complexity theory, *Education 3–13*, i*First*, 259– 269.

Holland, J.H. (1987) The global economy as an adaptive process. In P.W. Anderson, K.J. Arrow and D. Pines (eds) *The Economy as an Evolving Complex System*, Santa Fe Institute Studies in the Sciences of Complexity, Vol. 5. Redwood City, CA: Addison-Wesley.

Jacobson, M.J. (2000) Butterflies, traffic jams and cheetahs: Problem solving and complex systems. Paper presented at the American Educational Research Association, New Orleans, Louisiana, USA, 21 April.

Jess, M., Atencio, M. and Thorburn, M. (2011) Complexity Theory: Supporting curriculum and pedagogy developments in Scottish Physical Education, *Sport, Education and Society*, 16(2): 179–199.

Jones, R. (2007) Coaching redefined: an everyday pedagogical endeavour, *Sport, Education and Society*, 12, 159–173.

Kirk, D. (2010) *Physical Education Futures*. London: Routledge.

Lewin, R. (1993) *Complexity: Life at the edge of chaos*. London: Phoenix.

Morrison, K. (2008) Educational philosophy and the challenge of Complexity Theory, *Educational Philosophy and Theory*, 40(1), 19–34.

Nelson, L.J. and Groom, R. (2012) The analysis of athletic performance: some practical and philosophical considerations, *Sport, Education and Society*, 17, 687–701.

Puddifoot, J. (2000) Some problems and possibilities in the study of dynamical social processes, *Journal for the Theory of Social Behaviour*, 30 (1), 79–97.

Roberts, S. (2014) Talking relative age effects: a fictional analysis based on scientific evidence, *Asia-Pacific Journal of Health, Sport and Physical Education*, 5(1), 55–66.

Santonus, M. (1998) Simple, Yet Complex [online]. Available from http://www.cio.com/ archive/enterprise/ 041598_qanda_content.html (accessed 4 November, 2009).

Selbie, P. and Clough, P. (2005) Talking early childhood education: fictional enquiry with historical figures, *Journal of Early Childhood Research*, 3, 115–126.

Sparkes, A.C. (2002) *Telling Tales in Sport and Physical Activity: A Qualitative Journey*. Champaign, IL: Human Kinetics.

Wheatley, M. (1999) *Leadership and the New Science: Discovering order in a chaotic world* (2nd edn). San Francisco: Berrett-Koehler Publishers.

Youngblood, M. (1997) *Life at the Edge of Chaos*. Dallas, TX: Perceval Publishing.

INDEX

afPE *see* Association for Physical Education
Afro-Caribbean children 125
Alexander, R. 65, 92, 94
anxiety 3, 84, 131
Association for Physical Education (afPE) 36, 115
Atencio, M. et al. 51
athletic activities: cult of athleticism 119–20; NCPE 1991 Key Stage 1 programme of study 18; NCPE 1991 Key Stage 2 programme of study 20; NCPE 1995 Key Stage 2 areas of activity 27; NCPE 1999 Key Stage 2 33; and primary teacher training 46
axial movements 66

Bailey, R. 105; et al. 9, 12, 36
balance 65, 66
Ball, S.J. 83, 92–3
Basic Moves 90, 95
Beck, U. 10, 11
Begley, P.T. 5
behaviourism 61–2
Billett, S. 51
biographisation of youth 11
Black Papers 17, 28
Blair, R. and Capel, S. 82–3
Blair government 28–9
BMA (British Medical Association) Physical Education committee 9
bridge building *see* transition management within PE

British Medical Association (BMA) Physical Education committee 9
Bunker, D. and Thorpe, R. 63

Cale, L.A. and Harris, J. 9
Cameron, David 38
Capel, S. 6, 120–1; and Whitehead, M. 5
capital 123–4; cultural 123; economic 123–4; physical 123; social 123
Cartesian duality 7
Casbon, C. 93
CFE (Curriculum for Excellence) strategy 37, 110–14
Chedzoy, S. 89, 94
Children's Act (2004) 103
choice, opportunities for 94
Church 10
class *see* social class
Claxton, G. 92
Coalition government 35
cognitive dissonance 62–4
communication skills 75
Compton, A. 91
Connell, R. 120
constructivism 64
continuing professional development (CPE) 48–51; and assessment 67; attempts at providing CPE for primary PE 48–9; difficulties with programmes 49–50
convergent discovery 60
convergent learning 64